THE WOR[...]
of a DISCIPLE

LIVING LIKE JESUS

The Walking with God Series

VOLUME 2

DON COUSINS AND
JUDSON POLING

ZONDERVAN®

CONTENTS

PREFACE

The *Walking with God Series* was developed as the core curriculum for small groups at Willow Creek Community Church in South Barrington, Illinois. The material here flows out of the vision and values of this dynamic and world-renowned ministry. In the early years of Willow Creek, small groups using these studies produced many of the leaders, both staff and volunteer, throughout the church.

Don Cousins, who at the time was associate pastor at Willow Creek, wrote the first draft of this material and used it with his own small group. After testing it there, he revised it and passed his notes to Judson Poling, who was the director of curriculum development. He edited and expanded the outlines, and then several pilot groups helped retool the material. After the pilot groups completed the studies, a team of leaders labored through a yearlong, line-by-line revision. The revisions became the original six-volume *Walking with God Series*. Since its first publication in 1992, the series has sold more than one million copies and has been translated into seven languages.

Thirty years later, the authors have reworked the six-book series and created this updated and condensed edition, now 42 sessions in two volumes (instead of 78 sessions in six books). However, while there are fewer sessions overall, the authors have made sure this adaptation is true to the original and retains the distinctives of that proven study. They believe this new version will reach a whole new generation of Christ-followers who seek to become mature disciples of Jesus. A small group that uses and completes *The Way of a Disciple: Walking with Jesus* and *The Work of a Disciple: Living Like Jesus* will lay a solid foundation for a lifelong walk with God.

PART 1

LIFE-CHANGING COMMUNITY

Most of us have felt some measure of frustration with the church. At times we can't help feeling that the Spirit-driven, culturally relevant body of Christ has become a confused and ineffective institution. The church has been attacked from the outside and compromised on the inside, and in many places it is showing signs of wear. Those of us with the courage to be honest realize we have even made the situation worse on occasion. It is true there *are* churches that have been faithful witnesses for Christ, but too many others have been put to sleep.

It's one thing to declare, "Things are bad." It's another to say, "Here's the way out." Anybody can criticize. We must go further than diagnose—we must revive. We need to not only discover the church but also discover our place in it. We need to discover what contributions we can make to the church so it can again become the beautiful bride of Christ that God intended.

People must *come together* to become the church, but it's rare to find members who come together to *give* and not just to *take*. Your small group is a perfect place to change this pattern. The first step toward "contributing to the work" can happen there. It is a place where you are able to experience not only the joy of the church in action but also feel the satisfaction of being players in God's great plan.

By committing to this study, you are opening yourself up to some profound changes. You will never be able to look at the church in the same way, nor will you see yourself as you have in the past. This reality is the wonder of the church, the blessing of using our gifts, the satisfaction of being a contributor—relationally, emotionally, financially. This realization is what it means to "discover" the church.

A NEW COMMUNITY

PERSONAL STUDY: Psalm 145; Ephesians 1:1–22
SCRIPTURE MEMORY: Colossians 3:17
ON YOUR OWN: Jesus' Mission and the Church

"One hundred religious persons knit into a unity by careful organization do not constitute a church any more than eleven dead men make a football team. The first requisite is life, always."
—A. W. TOZER

God's People

Having just moved to a new city, Daryl and Ruth were anxious to find a new church. They had written a list of "musts" their church had to have—dynamic preaching and teaching, excellent music, a top-notch educational program, and activities for their children. But actually finding a church that met these qualifications was far more difficult than they imagined. Some churches they visited had great speakers but almost nothing for the youth. Others provided wonderful music in their worship services but had no commitment to evangelism or outreach.

Finally, after weeks of searching, Daryl and Ruth found what they were seeking. What ultimately tipped the scales for them was not what they originally expected. A sense of community existed among the members in this church that was infectious, and Daryl and Ruth realized this church was experiencing not only relevant teaching but also relevant living. This was a group they could worship with. These were people they could enjoy serving alongside. This was a place they could invite unchurched friends to attend without embarrassment. This was a community they could call home. They had found—and wanted to be part of—"the church."

Like Daryl and Ruth, we must keep in mind that the church ultimately is God's people—not a building, a pastor, or even the special programs that we commonly think of when we hear the word *church*. This study will show you some of the biblical teaching that lays out how God intended the church to function.

Life in My Church

1. What are two words or phrases that best describe your church experience growing up? Explain your answer.

2. What was the greatest positive contribution the church made to your life as you grew up?

3. What was your church experience lacking as you grew up?

4. In recent years, what are two to three ways the church has made a contribution to your life?

5. If you could no longer be a part of a church body, what would you really miss?

6. In recent years, what are two significant ways you have contributed to your church (other than financially)?

7. If you are unable to identify meaningful contributions you have made, what do you think is getting in the way?

Life in the First Church

8. *Read Acts* 2:38–47. What did Peter instruct the people to do (see verse 38)?

9. What promise did he give if they responded to his message (see verses 38–39)?

10. What happened as a result of Peter's words (see verse 41)?

11. To what did these new believers devote themselves (see verse 42)?

12. What did the presence of miracles and signs indicate (see verse 43)?

13. What strikes you as you read about their newfound priorities (see verses 44–46)?

14. How did the Lord bless these believers' efforts (see verse 47)?

15. In what ways is your church similar or different from this early group of believers?

16. To what extent do you think we should be copying these practices from the early church's experience in our day? Explain.

Your Walk with God

Central to the values behind this series is the belief that regular appointments with God will serve your spiritual life better in the long run than doing fill-in-the-blank "homework" related to the small-group study. Therefore, in this curriculum, your walk with God *is* the homework. Considering the pace of modern life, we thought it impractical for the average person to complete lengthy assignments to prepare for group meetings *and* have quiet times. For this reason, the material in this section was designed to help you establish simple foundational practices to enable you to maintain a vital connection with God.

Bible

Schedule three times this week to be alone with God. Pick the time during the day that works best for you. Each day, read the passage indicated below, write down one idea for application, and make a list of your observations from your study. Also, read over the article in the "On Your Own" section that follows.

DAY ONE: PSALM 145

Choose a verse of adoration from this psalm and meditate on its content. Some observations about the verse and how I can apply it to my life:

Two benefits I receive from meditating on this passage:

DAY TWO: EPHESIANS 1:1–14

Some observations about this passage and how I can apply it to my life:

Identify three sins you committed this past week. Some actions I need to take to make things right (other than claiming God's forgiveness):

DAY THREE: EPHESIANS 1:15–22

Some observations about this passage and how I can apply it to my life:

Some things God loves, based on the passage:

Prayer

Spend a few minutes praying about things that come to mind during your Bible reading. Pray specifically that God will increase your love for those things you've noted in this lesson. At the end of the week, list two or three benefits you received from these appointments with God.

Scripture Memory

As part of the curriculum, we've included memory verses with each lesson. If you desire to make this discipline part of your discipleship experience, begin by memorizing this verse:

> *And whatever you do, whether in word or deed, do it all in the name of the Lord Jesus, giving thanks to God the Father through him* (Colossians 3:17).

Next time, we will look at why the modern church has often failed to make much of an impact on the world. To prepare, think about what qualities the church in Acts 2 and 4 possessed, and in what ways the church today fails to resemble the New Testament church.

On Your Own: Jesus' Mission and the Church

What is the *proof* that Jesus accomplished his mission while on earth—that he, in fact, did what his Father sent him to do? The evidence most Christians point to is Jesus' sacrificial death for their sins and his resurrection from the dead. Surely those two events show his mission was a success. Or they point to Jesus' amazing teachings that were later written down in the Gospels. Even two thousand years later, his words encourage, convict, and delight people from all over the world. That must surely establish his divinely appointed legacy.

But what Christians often overlook among Jesus' greatest accomplishments is the fact that he took a ragtag band of men and women and mentored them to the point where they would become the beginning of a new community—a new nation of Israel, so to speak—who would take his message to the world. He was able to inspire and develop them so they continued his work in a climate of opposition and even persecution. This was a truly remarkable achievement.

Yes, Jesus left behind life-changing teachings and an empty grave. But he also brought into being an interconnected body of followers who modeled his new way of living. How they treated each other—along with what they taught—provides evidence that Jesus succeeded in his mission. As Jesus prayed in John 17:22–23, their "oneness" was part of the proof given to the watching world that God had sent him: "I have given them the glory that you gave me, that they may be one as we are one—I in them and you in me—so that they may be brought to complete unity. *Then the world will know that you sent me*" (emphasis added).

Power to Be Different—and Make a Difference

After Jesus rose from the dead, he appeared among his followers for about a month and a half and told them to wait in Jerusalem "for the gift my Father promised" (see Acts 1:1–5). He had charged them to go into all the world to make disciples, "baptizing them in the name of the Father and of the Son and of the Holy Spirit" (Matthew 28:19). But Jesus had one more bit of preparation to do in them before they headed out.

What was left on the agenda—the final step they needed before "graduating" from his training school—was to receive the gift of the Holy Spirit. Only after the Spirit arrived and filled them would they be ready. That would be the final step of gestation that would result in the birth of the church (see Acts 2). With the Spirit's help, they could have the full unity, purpose, and power they needed to carry on Jesus' mission.

As promised, the Holy Spirit did come in a way they could not mistake for anything other than a supernatural occurrence. But beyond the miraculous signs that were immediately evident, the Holy Spirit transformed them into a caring, loving community. The book of Acts describes a close-knit group of men and women who learned together, ate together, and even shared their resources when needed. They took care of one another in every way imaginable.

Because of the way they treated each other, the world now had added evidence that God sent Jesus. And what was even more exciting was that Jesus' mission was continuing to be fulfilled through them.

Why the Church?

Why is this oneness so crucial to God's program? If all he wants to do is get out a message, why not just broadcast it 24/7 through loudspeakers set up all over the world? What is the point of God entrusting a group of people—the church, with all its limitations—to do this vital work?

While it's not the whole answer, surely one of the main reasons for the church to be God's "speakers" is because God is all about community. A group of people is a much better mouthpiece for God's kind of truth than any other medium. People banding together reflect God's communal (Trinitarian) nature. In fact, you could say the whole Bible is a story of God working by calling and shaping a group of people to do his work. Not just one person was to be his representative—but a whole nation. In the Old Testament, it was Israel. In the New Testament, it is the church. God consistently uses a community of people to take his saving work to the rest of the world.

Beyond the twelve Jesus designated as apostles, he gathered an even larger group of men and women who followed him, supported him financially (see Luke 8:1–3), and were sent out to preach (see 10:1–24). Jesus designed his work to show that God's kingdom was a community. Think about it this way: Jesus taught his followers to pray, "Give us today our daily bread" (Matthew 6:11), not "Give *me* this day *my* daily bread." He had in mind a praying *community*—not just individuals—coming to God.

A Community Focused on One Another

In Paul's letters, he often gives instructions that include the words *one another*. He admonishes the church to love one another (see Romans 12:10), encourage one another (see 1 Thessalonians 5:11), build one another up (see Romans 15:2), and so on. Obviously, we cannot live "one-another" lives by ourselves! We can fulfill those commands only by being connected in meaningful ways with others in the body of Christ.

When English readers see the word *you* in the New Testament, they tend to think of it as singular. But the Greek language of the original text makes a distinction between *you* as one person and *you* a group of people. In Paul's writings, his admonitions are almost always plural. Community is assumed. It is the means through which we experience God's love, comfort, reassurance, and teaching. It is a way in which Jesus is always with us.

Who Was the Church For?

When Jesus chose his original twelve disciples, he included only men of Jewish descent. However, while the church began with these Jewish followers of Jesus, it quickly expanded to include Gentiles—people outside the circle of what had traditionally been seen as "God's people." Anyone who wanted to follow Jesus was welcomed. Any religious background, any gender, any social status, and any nationality.

The church brought together a diverse cross section of society into one group. In that part of the world, those people might never have talked to each other—or, if they did converse, they wouldn't have gotten along. But as they came together to seek God, they became unified. They also reached out to friends and family to share the good news with them. The result was that thousands (and eventually millions) of people who were far from God were drawn to him through the church.

Today, Jesus' mission is still the same: to challenge people who might otherwise not get along to live as one body and show the world how much power there is in the gospel. If we fail to do that, the message will lose some of its power.

Yet if we live as one, we show the world that Jesus and the Father are One. If we give rather than just take, we show the world that God is a giver and not a taker. If we love one another across racial, political, and socioeconomic divides, we show that God loves everyone and wants everyone in his kingdom. If we become known for the things we are *for* instead of what we are *against*, we reflect the winsomeness, kindness, and welcoming nature of God. What we do in this world, he is doing. What we fail to do will be a hole in the gospel that prevents people from seeing Jesus more clearly.

Now, as in the first century, we—the worldwide church in loving action—are the "proof" that Jesus accomplished his earthly mission. We are also the means by which he *continues* to fulfill it for each new generation.

STRAIGHT TALK ABOUT THE CHURCH

PERSONAL STUDY: Ephesians 2:1–9, 11–22
SCRIPTURE MEMORY: 1 Corinthians 14:12
ON YOUR OWN: Change Within the Church

"For his own unfathomable reasons, God chooses to disguise himself when he comes to this planet, and there have been few disguises better than the church."
—MARK GALLI

Inconsiderate Neighbors

Tired of having to pay for expensive tools every time you want to do home repairs and yard work, you call your neighbors together and announce that you want to start a tool-lending cooperative. Like you, they each have several items that are necessary for handiwork. Now, together, you have virtually all the equipment you need to do most repairs and projects. Your neighbors enthusiastically agree to participate, and the venture gets started.

On the first weekend, a few neighbors take a share of your tools for things they need to do around their homes. Although you wanted to fix a few things of your own, you decide to be generous—and patient—and wait until the next weekend to get your tools back. But when that time arrives, no one is ready to return your tools. Worse still, when you want to borrow their tools, they tell you that you can't because they are going to use them that day. This continues for months. After all that time of not being able borrow anything, and with your items still in everyone else's garages, you angrily realize this arrangement is a colossal failure.

When it comes to serving their church, many Christians are like these inconsiderate neighbors. They are glad to take what they can out of a local body but are reluctant to contribute to its well-being. This study will help you understand three present-day obstacles that hinder the church's effectiveness.

1. *Read Acts 4:32–37.* How did the believers in the New Testament church act toward one another? What was the result?

2. In what ways does the church today resemble the New Testament church?

3. In what ways does the church today fail to resemble the New Testament church?

4. Why do you think the church today falls short when measured up against the New Testament church?

Enemies of the Modern Church

There are three main enemies of the modern church that hamper its effectiveness: (1) our culture's rugged individualism, (2) ineffective spiritual leadership within the church, and (3) our society's consumer mentality. We will consider each of these enemies in this study.

Rugged Individualism

5. In what ways has the rugged individualism of our culture affected the way you regard your wealth and possessions?

6. *Read Acts 4:32–37 again.* How did these early Christians regard their wealth and possessions?

7. How has rugged individualism affected your participation in the church?

8. What are some simple things you can do to be less individualistic?

Ineffective Spiritual Leadership

9. Why is effective spiritual leadership important for every church?

10. *Read Hebrews 13:17.* How does this verse describe effective spiritual leadership?

11. What does this verse say is your role in supporting your spiritual leaders?

12. Without having a judgmental spirit, in what ways could you help the leaders in your church become more effective in their service?

The Consumer Mentality

13. Why do you think the consumer mentality is so prevalent among many Christians?

14. *Read 2 Corinthians 8:1–7.* How did Paul commend the churches in Macedonia?

15. How would you contrast the "grace of giving" found in these Macedonian churches with the attitude of many Christians in churches today?

16. How can you become less of a consumer and more of a giver?

Apply It to Your Life

17. What are some specific steps you can take so you become a more active participant in your church?

Your Walk with God

Bible

Schedule three times this week to be alone with God. Each day, read the passage indicated below and answer the questions that follow.

DAY ONE: EPHESIANS 2:1–9

Some of the things I observe in this passage:

One idea for how to apply this passage to my life:

DAY TWO: EPHESIANS 2:11–16

Some of the things I observe in this passage:

One idea for how to apply this passage to my life:

DAY THREE: EPHESIANS 2:17–22

Some of the things I observe in this passage:

One idea for how to apply this passage to my life:

Prayer

On each of your three days with God this week, pray for the following:

Day One: Meditate on Psalm 37:1–11. Consider all the promises God gives to us in these verses.

Day Two: Think of some things that come to mind for which you can thank God. One by one, bring them to him in prayer.

Day Three: Think of one quality you see in the life of another believer that you would like to have in your own life and pray about that today.

List some changes that you want God to begin making in you:

Scripture Memory

Memorize this verse this week:

Since you are eager for gifts of the Spirit, try to excel in those that build up the church (1 Corinthians 14:12).

Next time, we will explore the Christian's role in the church. To prepare for the session, read 1 Corinthians 12:1–31; Ephesians 5:21–23; 1 Peter 2:1–12; and Ephesians 4:1–16.

On Your Own: Change Within the Church

Although the church today looks different than it did during the first century, that doesn't necessarily mean those differences are all bad. Two thousand years ago, that church—like ours—was full of problems too. Our goal is not to reproduce the church of Acts in our day. Rather, our goal is to be the church God wants—taking the best of what we read in the book of Acts while avoiding the mistakes they made.

When the local church is "working right," it really is a thing of beauty and a light to the surrounding culture. When the church is welcoming, offers sound teaching, reaches out to the poor, and helps people discover and use their spiritual gifts, it can have an amazing impact on the people within it and the world around it. It can be a place where people find God and experience his love.

How Has the Church Gotten Off Track?

Yet the church has had a "colorful" history (to say the least!). There have been times of sacrificial, Christ-honoring ministry but also embarrassing eras of terrible non-Christlike behavior. We, the church historical, have both blessed the world in the name of Jesus and damaged his name before the world.

Here are just a few examples of how the church can get—and has gotten—off track:

- Leaders vie for power instead of humbly serving others.
- People want the church to share resources with them, but they aren't willing to share their own resources with the church.
- People want to be fed but won't apply what they've been taught.
- Churches become closed or cliquish instead of welcoming.
- The teaching is pabulum and ineffectual, or conversely judgmental and soul-crushing.
- Entertainment is put before truth.
- Truth is used as a weapon and dispensed without grace.
- The poor are ignored and the rich are coddled.
- All the work gets done by just a few.
- Congregants become consumers instead of co-laborers.
- People are unchanged after years of attending—and nobody seems to think that's a problem.

The church needs to be a place where people shine their light and draw others to God (see Matthew 5:14–16). This is not done through clever gimmicks or impressive programs but through authentic love for one another and for whoever walks through the door.

As you consider this, think about whether you find yourself believing it's somebody else's problem. Have you just read all the above and said, "I'm sure glad I'm not that way!" That's what most people do, and that's why nothing changes! We're prone to focus on everybody else's faults instead of asking, "What are *my* blind spots—how do *I* need to change?" Jesus warned us that the plank is in our *own* eye (see Matthew 7:3). As long as we keep talking about the speck we see in everybody else's eye, we won't function the way Jesus wants us to.

What Needs to Change?

Here are some ideas for how we can approach this differently:

- If we are disappointed with the church, we need to see that changing the church means changing ourselves and being a force for change within our local community.

- If we want our church to be "deeper" spiritually, we need to cultivate that in ourselves and be willing to engage in more honest conversations.

- If we want our church to minister to the poor, or feed the hungry, or visit prisoners (as Jesus told us we should in Matthew 25:35–40), then we need to do those things.

- Rather than waiting for our church to start a program, we can propose or even launch an initiative. We need to be the change we wish to see in the church.

How does this happen? One simple suggestion is to begin with whatever bothers you the most, as you'll be more motivated to change those things you care about. So, what problem in the world or in your church drives you crazy? Maybe your concern is just the thing God is using to nudge you into action. Perhaps God has placed a "holy discontent" in your heart to motivate you to be a difference-maker. And maybe he wants you to invite some other like-minded people to join you so his light will shine in the darkness.

MORE THAN A BUILDING

PERSONAL STUDY: Psalm 8; Ephesians 3
SCRIPTURE MEMORY: 1 Corinthians 12:27
ON YOUR OWN: Unity and Belonging

"We've been given the covenant community because we need each other, and together we'll be more mature, experience more life, and know more joy than we ever would apart from one another."

—Matt Chandler

Understanding Our Importance

At the base of the human brain is a small organ called the pituitary gland. By appearances, it wouldn't seem to be a big contributor to the overall function of the human body. But in recent times, scientists have discovered this tiny gland is a vital regulator. It secretes necessary hormones that are transported to other organs. Along with the nervous system, it coordinates and integrates those mechanisms that help us adapt to changes in our environment. It can also "tell" other glands to produce greater quantities of hormones. It is very small, but the body could not function properly without it.

Christians sometimes don't understand the importance of *their* part in the body of Christ. They agree in principle that they should be serving others and participating in the life of the church, but their actions belie their commitment. Some feel they do not have gifts of any importance—that God doesn't need them to do his work in the world. Others believe they are not as worthy as others; and so being unqualified, they presume God will not use them. Whatever the excuse, Christians who remain on the sidelines not only miss out on the benefits of active service but also frustrate God's attempts to use them in a manner pleasing to him.

By looking at four New Testament passages during this study, we will see how the early church was encouraged to serve one another. In this lesson we will focus on 1 Corinthians 12:1–31; Ephesians 5:21–23; 1 Peter 2:1–12; and Ephesians 4:1–16. This study will show you how God wants you to function as a member of the body of Christ and how the church is held together in Christ.

The Body of Christ

1. Have one person read 1 Corinthians 12:1–31 aloud. What important truth should Christians keep in mind when they talk about their spiritual gifts (see verses 4–6)?

2. How can we feel confident that God will use the gifts he has given us (see verses 18–19)? What reassurance did Paul give to Christians who don't feel their roles and contributions are important (see verses 22–25)?

3. Write a paraphrase of verse 26. When have you suffered because a part of the body of Christ was suffering?

4. Why are some gifts more desirable than others (see verse 31)?

The Bride of Christ

5. *Turn to Ephesians 5:21–23.* Why are we to submit to one another?

6. Why do you think Paul chose the illustration of marriage to describe Christ's relationship to the church?

A Building of People

A lone brick has virtually no value. Tossed by itself in the front yard, it is useless, even a nuisance. If it is placed in the street, it will get run over and worn out. It may even do damage to whatever car or bike encounters it. But a brick properly positioned in a wall functions according to design and is supported and sustained by adjacent bricks. If each brick is placed with the others according to the architect's plans, it results in a useful and beautiful structure.

This analogy describes the role of Christians in the church. When they purposefully decide to go it alone, they are usually ineffective and can actually do harm to the body of Christ. However, when they are interconnected and interacting with other believers, they help each other and fulfill God's purpose.

Living Stones

7. *Turn to 1 Peter 2:1–12.* Of what are believers to rid themselves (see verse 1)?

8. Why are Christians supposed to crave spiritual milk (see verse 2)?

9. What is significant about believers being built into a house (see verse 5)?

10. Why has God given such special status to his people (see verse 9)?

11. What effect does living a good life among unbelievers have on them (see verse 12)?

The Mortar—Unity in Christ

12. *Now turn to Ephesians 4:1–16.* What are the characteristics of Christians who are living lives pleasing to God (see verse 2)?

13. What two goals should all who are in the body strive for (see verses 11–13)?

14. How will unity in the body of Christ protect believers (see verse 14)?

15. Why is Christ's lordship necessary to the growth of the body (see verses 15–16)?

16. How does your spiritual condition affect the health of the rest of the body (see verse 16)? What do you believe is the effect you are having these days?

Your Walk with God

Bible

Schedule three times this week to be alone with God. Each day, read the passage indicated below and answer the questions that follow.

DAY ONE: PSALM 8

Choose a verse from this psalm and meditate on its content. Some observations about the verse and how I can apply it to my life:

My prayer of thanksgiving for the many ways God has shown his grace to me:

DAY TWO: EPHESIANS 3:1–13

Some of the things I observe in this passage:

One idea for how to apply this passage to my life:

DAY THREE: EPHESIANS 3:14–21

Some of the things I observe in this passage:

One idea for how to apply this passage to my life:

Prayer

On each of your three days with God this week, pray for the following:

Day One: Confess any sins that have troubled you more than usual in recent days. Thank God for allowing you to approach him in freedom and confidence (as noted in Ephesians 3:12).

Day Two: Identify three people for whom you can pray, using Paul's words in Ephesians 3:14–21 as a model. Be specific in your requests on their behalf.

Day Three: Pray specifically for each member of your family.

Scripture Memory

Memorize this verse this week:

> *Now you are the body of Christ, and each one of you is a part of it*
> (1 Corinthians 12:27).

In the next study, we will look at some practical ways we can encourage others and make contributions to the body of Christ. To prepare, ask yourself in what ways you currently contribute to the church. Are you more of a giver or a taker? In what areas could you improve your service to other Christians? Also meditate on Hebrews 10:24–25 and consider what motivates you to love God and others more.

On Your Own: Unity and Belonging

Like many things of beauty, unity among believers is a wonder to behold but also rare and fragile. Our human nature tends to be self-focused. We like the idea of unity, but our actions and attitudes reflect the fact that we also like doing our own thing. Another way to say it is that we have a strong propensity to be selfish. This is human nature in action, just as Paul describes in Romans 7:5–20.

To get to unity, we cannot just try harder. We must be changed on the inside, through Christ. Our transformation, both individually and collectively, is what makes the church into what it's supposed to be.

Paul described the church as a *body*—it's a living entity. As such, it's better to think of it as an *organism* rather than an *organization*. We are by design interconnected and interdependent (see 1 Corinthians 12:12–31). When each of us plays our role, we accomplish together what none of us could alone. But we do far more: we create a bond that allows us to experience a deeply satisfying sense of belonging. We become a part of something larger than ourselves, and seeing it inspires us. Together, we experience God in ways we could not on our own.

How do we develop this unity and interconnection? The Bible says it begins with humility and submission to Christ and then to each other (see Ephesians 5:21). Submission is not becoming a doormat, nor is humility self-degradation. Rather, God calls us to a right-sized view of ourselves and to make ourselves less of a focus. Paul says it succinctly in Romans 12:3: "Do not think of yourself more highly than you ought."

We cannot have unity if we keep focusing on ourselves. Unity requires humility and putting others first (see Philippians 2:3). It sometimes requires sacrifice, surrendering our desires and preferences for the good of the whole body. This requires not so much thinking less of ourselves but rather thinking of ourselves less.

It's also true that each of us is important and valuable. We all bring a contribution to the body. If instead of thinking of ourselves less, we go too far and think of ourselves as *nothing*, the church will miss out on the blessings we are able to bring. Our God-given gifts will be absent from the mix.

We must cultivate the ability to see others as God sees them—equally loved, equally valued, equally gifted. Each person has a part to play. Even if someone has what we judge to be a limited contribution, the very fact that God wants him or her to bring it means it's important.

A repeated theme of the New Testament is unity and connection. Look at Ephesians 4:2–6 and notice how often the word *one* comes up: "Be completely humble and gentle; be patient, bearing with *one* another in love. Make every effort to keep the unity of the Spirit through the bond of peace. There is *one* body and *one* Spirit, just as you were called to *one* hope when you were called; *one* Lord, *one* faith, *one* baptism; *one* God and Father of all, who is over all and through all and in all" (emphasis added).

The Greek word translated as "one another" (*allelon*) is found one hundred times in the Bible. Paul's letters exhort us to bear with one another, encourage one another, love one another, and so on (see, for example, Ephesians 4:2; 4:32; and 5:21). Christianity is a "one another" faith. That's a major way the love of God gets expressed to all of us within the church and to an outside world desperate for his love. And when we need an infusion of God's goodness, the community of other people is one of the best ways to get it. That interconnection between us—in all of its messy glory—is also what continues to form us into the image of Christ.

THE POWER OF ENCOURAGEMENT

PERSONAL STUDY: Ephesians 4–6
SCRIPTURE MEMORY: Philippians 2:3; Hebrews 10:25
ON YOUR OWN: How to Build Up Others

"Be kind, for everyone you meet is fighting a great battle."

—PHILO OF ALEXANDRIA

Be Encouraged

Is there someone in your life you would call an encourager—someone who gives your spirit a lift with kind, supportive words? All of us can remember times in our lives when another person's words helped us through a trying situation or bolstered our self-worth—perhaps during the loss of a loved one, a difficult time at work or school, or even after a bad day. Encouragers also help us keep our perspective by reminding us of truths that we may have forgotten or ignored.

Such people are acutely needed in the church! The New Testament is filled with examples of believers who demonstrated an active caring for needy or discouraged brothers and sisters in the faith. In fact, different forms of the word *encourage* appear thirty-seven times in the New Testament.

During this study, you will put the practical knowledge you have learned about the church to work by doing an exercise that will help you build up others in the church. You will also examine the importance of making a contribution to the body of Christ through your relationships. And you will look at Hebrews 10:24–25 to gain an in-depth perspective on what fellowship in the church is all about.

Encouragement in the Early Church

1. *Read Acts 18:27.* How did the brothers and sisters assist Apollos in his effort to go to Achaia?

2. What general principle about encouragement can you draw from this short passage?

Working Together

A high school baseball team is enthusiastic about its chances for the city championship. They have good team defense, and their offense is a potent mix of power and speed. The pitching staff is as good as any around. But the team has a big problem: its star shortstop is threatening to quit the team unless he can bat fourth in the lineup and pitch every third game.

Angry and puzzled, the team holds a conference to decide what to do. The shortstop isn't a good enough hitter to hit cleanup. And he's more valuable as a shortstop than as a pitcher. The team desperately needs his contribution—but on the infield defense, not where he is so stubbornly demanding to be positioned. After long but fruitless talks, the player quits the team. His choice becomes all the more painful when the team loses in the semifinal round—all because of an error made by the replacement shortstop.

In the church, we all depend on one another. We all need to develop caring hearts and people-oriented outlooks that enable the church to work as a united team.

3. *Read Philippians 2:1–2.* What benefits do we receive from our union with Christ?

4. In what ways were these believers to be like-minded? In what ways have you recently shown Christ's love to other members in your church?

5. How might you have allowed your own concerns to override your consideration for other believers? What can you do to correct that issue?

6. *Now read Philippians 2:3–4.* Why do you think Paul cautioned these Christians not to do things out of "selfish ambition or vain conceit"? Why is it necessary to consider others better than yourself?

7. Was there ever a time when someone practiced these principles to your benefit? Explain.

8. Who in your life could benefit from a more selfless attitude on your part?

Living Coals

A long time ago, a country pastor paid a visit to a man in his congregation. This man attended church infrequently, always finding excuses to stay home or do other activities. As they talked about the man's pattern of missing services, the pastor walked over to the fireplace, picked up the tongs, and removed a coal from the fire. Then he placed it by itself on the hearth and returned to the conversation.

The man thought the pastor's action strange, but as they talked, the force of the illustration hit home. The pastor explained, "Missing one service is not going to kill you any more than removing that one coal from the fire will immediately put it out. But if we wait a while, that coal is going to grow cold, and eventually the flame will go out completely. The longer you stay away from church and fellow believers, the dimmer your light will become. And notice the rest of the coals still in the fire: they are burning brightly together and are warm. They can offer us comfort on this cold day. But that one coal? It's 'alive,' if you can call it that, but it's basically useless for what a fire is supposed to do."

As a body of believers, we are "living coals." We are designed to burn brightest when brought together in close association; separated from others, our flame will go out. It isn't just a bad idea to live unconnected from other Christians, but it's also a violation of God's plan and hazardous to our long-term spiritual health.

Spurring On One Another

Read Hebrews 10:24–25 and examine each of the following phrases from the passage.

9. *"And let us consider . . ."* The word *consider* means "to mull over, plan, or think about." What were the main things you considered this week? How does what you consider in this way reveal key aspects of who you are as a person and what you value?

10. *"How we may spur one another . . ."* When has something spurred you on to action recently? What was your mental and emotional state?

11. *"On toward love . . ."* What inspires you or spurs you on to love God more? What spurs you on to love others?

12. *"And good deeds . . ."* When was a time that someone stirred you to do good deeds?

13. *"Not giving up meeting together . . ."* What tempts you to skip out on times when Christians meet together?

14. *"As some are in the habit of doing . . ."* What could you do to challenge someone who doesn't regard participation in a church or small group as being important?

15. *"But encouraging one another—and all the more as you see the Day approaching."* What is meant by "the Day"? Why is that a factor in this context?

An Exercise in Encouragement: The "Appreciation Hot Seat"

In this exercise, you will take turns expressing appreciation for each person in your group. One person will sit in the "hot seat" first, and then everyone will complete the sentences below with a word or phrase about that person. When all members have spoken their four phrases of appreciation for the person, the next person will sit in the "hot seat," and you will repeat the process. Continue until everyone has had a chance to be appreciated by all. If you have time constraints, you can also do this exercise by appreciating only the person on your right (with these four phrases), and then go around the circle to your left, giving each person a chance to appreciate the person on his or her right.

Some positive character traits I've noticed about you are _____.

One incident I remember that made me appreciate you more was _____.

One quality about your character that I could use more of is _____.

Our group would be missing the following if you weren't here: _____.

Your Walk with God

Bible

Schedule three times this week to be alone with God. Each day, read the passage indicated below and answer the questions that follow.

DAY ONE: EPHESIANS 4:1–32

Some of the things I observe in this passage:

One idea for how to apply this passage to my life:

DAY TWO: EPHESIANS 5:1–33

Some of the things I observe in this passage:

One idea for how to apply this passage to my life:

DAY THREE: EPHESIANS 6:1–24

Some of the things I observe in this passage:

One idea for how to apply this passage to my life:

Prayer

On each of your three days with God this week, pray for the following:

Day One: Pray that God will develop in you those qualities that will build up the church, such as humbleness, gentleness, patience, and bearing with one another (see Ephesians 4:2). Pray that the Holy Spirit will prepare and mature the people in your church for works of service.

Day Two: Look at your calendar for the upcoming week. Pray for each event and appointment, including family times. Consider how the Holy Spirit's presence in your life has affected you, and then give thanks to God.

Day Three: Thank God that he has included you as a part of his church. Confess the times you have hindered the work of your church and pray for any corporate needs in your church body.

Scripture Memory

Memorize these verses this week:

> *Do nothing out of selfish ambition or vain conceit. Rather, in humility*
> *value others above yourselves* (Philippians 2:3).

> *And let us not neglect our meeting together, as some people do, but encourage*
> *one another, especially now that the day of his return is drawing near*
> (Hebrews 10:25 NLT).

Next time, the group will participate in another relational exercise. Prepare by thinking about character traits you would like to change about yourself or that you have struggled with lately.

On Your Own: How to Build Up Others

Words have enormous power. Ask others to tell you a story of what has shaped them into the people they are today, and they will doubtless recount a conversation that marked them—either in a positive way or a negative way.

Encouraging words can change the direction of people's lives. They can bring people hope in the midst of despair and even inspire them to do more than they thought they were capable of doing. Because of this power, God commands all of us to "encourage one another and build each other up" (1 Thessalonians 5:11).

When we build others up, we are also being built up. If we become healthier in one part of our physical body, it will likely improve our overall health. So it is in the church: when we encourage one person, that person is empowered and strengthened to impact others in a positive way, and the whole body benefits. Encouragement given eventually becomes encouragement received because of our interconnection.

So, how can we become better at encouraging others and "build one another up"? Here are three practical ways:

1. Be Specific

Rather than just saying, "Wow, you're terrific," be specific about what you see in the people you're trying to encourage. How is God using them? What strengths do you see?

Catch them doing something right and tell them exactly what you saw. You might say, "I noticed you welcoming new people into our group," or "I can clearly see that you have a gift of mercy because you seem to know just how to comfort and support people when they're suffering."

Name the specific actions and attitudes rather than offering vague support. Start your encouragement with phrases like "I really like the way you . . ." or "One thing I really appreciate about you is . . ." and then just fill in the rest.

2. Be Immediate

When people are discouraged, be present with them—physically and emotionally. Don't stand at a distance or put off the opportunity to encourage them in that moment. Even if you feel uncomfortable with their pain, be brave and move toward them. As the Bible tells us, "A word fitly spoken is like apples of gold in settings of silver" (Proverbs 25:11 NKJV). It's less important what you say than it is just to offer yourself—and the "right time" is as soon as possible!

The same thing applies when people have done something worthy of commendation. If you wait too long, you may forget what you saw. They may also grow fuzzy about what happened. But if you speak up quickly—even if it's just a few words—your encouragement will build up their faith and motivate them to keep taking steps in a positive direction.

3. Be Confident

In this context, confidence is not so much being sure you know what you're saying is actually true as it is about being so secure in yourself that other people's accomplishments don't threaten you. It will be a lot harder to appreciate others if you think their being good makes you look bad, or that if you appreciate them, no one will appreciate you. When you are confident in the adequacy of your own strengths and gifts, you'll find it easier to affirm others.

You cannot manufacture this confidence by positive thinking or pretending. You must keep focusing your thoughts on Jesus and how much he loves you. When you fill your heart and mind with the truth of God's love for you, it will be easier to give to others.

THE CHALLENGE OF FOLLOWING

PERSONAL STUDY: Romans 14; Philemon
SCRIPTURE MEMORY: 1 John 5:3–4
ON YOUR OWN: Courage to Follow and Be Accountable

"You are what you do, not what you say you'll do."
—C. G. JUNG

Heart to Heart

Many of our contacts with people on a daily basis are superficial. Given the pace of life, we tend to avoid sharing deeper concerns. Then too, many people don't really expect a truthful answer to "How are you?" and other such pleasantries. In your small group, however, this sense of superficiality should gradually be replaced with a deeper sense of friendship. It is sad to have a small group that studies and prays together but doesn't build genuine and caring relationships.

This meeting will provide an opportunity for your group to share on a deeper level. Please note that the sharing shouldn't be forced. No one should feel compelled to talk about something he or she isn't ready to talk about. But we do encourage you to participate willingly, especially in light of the principles we'll be studying in this lesson. During this lesson, you will also examine what it means to be accountable to God and to spiritual leaders.

Bearing Burdens

1. *Read Galatians 6:2.* What does it mean to carry another's burdens?

2. *Read Romans 15:1–2.* Why is it helpful to share struggles in your small group?

Clothed with Compassion

3. *Turn to Colossians 3:12–17.* How are you to bear with and forgive others?

4. What else do you see in these verses that would build intimacy between people?

Being Accountable

To whom are you accountable? If you think about it, you are accountable to many people. If you are a student, you are accountable to the teacher to complete your work. If you are a taxpayer, you are accountable to the government and all your other fellow citizens to pay your taxes. If you are driving a car, you are accountable to law enforcement agencies and other drivers to obey traffic laws. If you rent an apartment, you are accountable to the landlord to pay the rent on time and to other tenants to be respectful about late-night noise.

There are endless other examples that could be produced, but they all illustrate the same point: like it or not, everyone has obligations to others that must be fulfilled. Yet some Christians are uncomfortable when it comes to sharing their lives and being accountable to other believers. Although they are willing to accept the fact they must be held accountable to other people and institutions, they are reluctant to allow themselves to be responsible to and for other believers. They do not stop to think about how many struggles with sin could be overcome if they received the counsel and encouragement of other Christians.

Accountability before God

5. *Read Matthew 12:35–37.* What did Jesus mean when he said you are accountable for your words? Why do you think your words are so important to God?

6. *Read Romans 14:10–12.* In what way is your judgment of others tied to your own accountability?

7. *Read Hebrews 9:27.* Why is it important to make your life count right now?

8. *Turn to 1 Corinthians 4:1–5.* How would you contrast accountability before God with standing before other people? Why should you not judge anything "before the appointed time"?

9. *Read 1 Corinthians 3:10–15.* What do these verses reveal about your accountability to God? What is the "wood, hay, or straw" in your life? What is the "gold, silver, costly stones"?

Accountability to Spiritual Leaders

10. *Read Hebrews 13:17.* What does this verse say about how you should respond to spiritual leadership? What responsibility do your church leaders have for you?

11. *Look up 1 Corinthians 16:13–16.* What qualifications should spiritual leaders possess?

12. What does it mean in practical terms to submit to your leaders? When is it right to refuse to submit to leaders?

Sharing Heart to Heart

In this next exercise, you will get a chance to take some risks and be vulnerable with each other. Note that some groups may be ready to dive deep as they share their answers to the following questions, while others may need to ease into this kind of self-revealing. Assure all group members that they are free to share at whatever level they are comfortable. The only challenge we offer is to take at least a small risk to let others know "the real you."

13. Putting all humility aside for a moment, I'd like to brag by telling you about . . .

14. Lately I've been preoccupied with thoughts about . . .

15. As I look closely at my life these days, I'm most concerned about . . .

16. If I could change one thing about my life, it would be . . .

17. The sin in my life that I find easy to rationalize away is . . .

18. I feel as though I have failed God and myself when this happens . . .

Your Walk with God

Bible

Schedule three times this week to be alone with God. Each day, read the passage indicated below and answer the questions that follow.

DAY ONE: ROMANS 14:1–12

Some of the things I observe in this passage:

One idea for how to apply this passage to my life:

DAY TWO: ROMANS 14:13–23

Some of the things I observe in this passage:

One idea for how to apply this passage to my life:

DAY THREE: PHILEMON 1–25

Some of the things I observe in this passage:

One idea for how to apply this passage to my life:

Prayer

On each of your three days with God this week, pray for the following:

Day One: Pray specifically for your example around new Christians and that they may come to a fuller relationship with God because of your actions.

Day Two: Pray for specific guidance on how to serve Christ in a way that is pleasing to God and approved by others (see Romans 14:18). Also pray for reconciliation between Christians in your church.

Day Three: Pray that God would show you where you need to be more accountable to him and be more accountable to your spiritual leaders.

Scripture Memory

Memorize these verses this week:

> *This is love for God: to keep his commands. And his commands are not burdensome, for everyone born of God overcomes the world* (1 John 5:3–4).

In the next lesson, we will continue to look at how believers in Christ are to be accountable to one another and how we are called to tell the truth and receive the truth from others. To prepare, think about a time when you observed something about another person but were too afraid to talk to him or her—and it led to unnecessary pain for that person. What kept you from speaking up? How might the person have responded if you had said something?

On Your Own: Courage to Follow and Be Accountable

Most of us know that leadership requires courage and character. However, there's another challenge we should be equally prepared to step up to: the challenge of *following well*. For those of us who like to lead, it can be hard to let go of being in charge. We have to open ourselves to accountability and humble ourselves enough to let someone else take charge or ask the tough questions.

As you've explored in this lesson, the life of faith includes being held accountable to God, to each other, and to your leaders. Each of these presents particular challenges. To help you in this, the following are three spiritual practices you can employ to help you be more honest and more willing to be accountable to others.

Practice 1: Self-Examination

Self-examination is a practice in which you take an honest inventory of your attitudes and actions, as guided by the Holy Spirit. It's important to remember that the Holy Spirit does not condemn you but wants to uncover patterns that are restricting your growth. The Bible promises there is no condemnation for those who are in Christ (see Romans 8:1). However, the Bible also teaches that you are to invite God to show you where you need to change or grow. As Psalm 139:23–24 states:

Search me, God, and know my heart; test me and know my anxious thoughts. See if there is any offensive way in me, and lead me in the way everlasting.

You can begin to practice self-examination by praying this psalm in its entirety and then asking God to show you, specifically, what is going well and what is hindering your growth. Another excellent passage to use in this practice is Galatians 5:16–26. Here you find two lists: (1) the "acts of the flesh," and (2) the "fruit of the Spirit." Read slowly through each list and honestly assess yourself, asking God to reveal the truth.

Are lust, rage, jealousy, and other acts of the flesh bringing you down? With which specific sins are you wrestling? Name them before God. Also, can you see the fruit of God's Spirit in your life? Are you more peaceful and joyful these days than you were a year ago? Can you point to recent actions where you've demonstrated patience, shown kindness, and acted with gentleness? Would others use any of these words to describe you?

The fruit of the Spirit is not a to-do list but rather a description of what your heart looks like when God is in control. A heart submitted to him will naturally "grow" these characteristics. In nature, an apple doesn't come from the tree putting forth *effort*—straining and striving to push an apple out on its branch! It comes from the tree being healthy and taking in water, sunshine, and nutrients—the fruit is simply the outgrowth of that process. Likewise, the fruit of the Spirit comes not from what you do for God—straining and striving to be those things—but from spending time in God's presence and allowing his power to operate in you.

Practice 2: Confession

Once you've spent some time in self-examination, your response should be to confess (agree with God about) "what you have done, and what you have left undone," as the ancient liturgy says. What acts of the flesh—those things toward which your human nature is drawn—have tempted you and tripped you up? Tell God about them and ask for his forgiveness. What spiritual fruit is not growing in your life?

What patterns are hindering that growth? Tell God about all of that and express your desire for patience, kindness, joy, or whatever else seems to be missing.

The Bible promises that if you confess your sins, God will forgive them. It is also clear that everyone sins—and that you are only fooling yourself if you say you don't. First John 1:8–10 gives us a warning, but also a promise:

> *If we claim to be without sin, we deceive ourselves and the truth is not in us. If we confess our sins, he is faithful and just and will forgive us our sins and purify us from all unrighteousness. If we claim we have not sinned, we make him out to be a liar and his word is not in us.*

Confession makes you right with God and actually helps you to avoid falling into the same patterns again. Naming your sin specifically, rather than simply praying, "Forgive me for messing up," will help you grow and strengthen your intimacy with God. Note that you don't list your sins to inform God—he already knows. The specificity is for your benefit. That honesty keeps you from rationalizations and cover-up and removes any barriers between you and God.

Practice 3: Worship

Once you've been honest with God, you can be assured he forgives and purifies you. Your response to this truth should be joyful worship. Telling God your sin and knowing he loves and forgives you should inspire you to praise him. Psalm 32 is a great guide for these steps of self-examination and confession, then worship:

> *Then I acknowledged my sin to you and did not cover up my iniquity. I said, "I will confess my transgressions to the LORD." And you forgave the guilt of my sin. Therefore let all the faithful pray to you while you may be found. . . . Rejoice in the LORD and be glad, you righteous; sing, all you who are upright in heart!* (verses 5–6, 11).

Such a process reminds you that God loves you despite your shortcomings, and he does not condemn you, but invites you into loving accountability. To know that when you confess your sin you are forgiven will cause you to rejoice. Such grace will prompt you to say thank you to God and inspire you to love in return the One who first loved you.

Accountability, Honesty, and Spiritual Growth

One of the paradoxes of our culture is that while it is easy to connect instantaneously with an almost limitless number of people electronically, we often are "alone" and anonymous. The vitriol we spill on social media can reach thousands of people, yet we do so without ever revealing anything about ourselves—even our name. We have countless methods of communication, and yet we can remain isolated and disconnected.

Being part of a church—and specifically part a small group with whom we meet regularly—can combat this isolation. Yet it will benefit us only if we choose to be honest in that setting. If we do not disclose our story, we aren't going to be known as we are. It will just be another place where we keep up appearances.

Our attempts at spiritual growth should not be a cloak that covers what is truly going on inside us. As Brené Brown observed, "Perfectionism is not the same thing as striving to be our best. Perfectionism is not about healthy achievement and growth; it's a shield." One of the best ways to give up that perfectionism is to admit what isn't perfect about us. The ironic thing is, while we may think we are telling people what is hidden from them, when we finally let down our guard, most will say they knew that about us anyway—they were just hoping we would finally admit it to ourselves!

Sharing our story—the good and the bad—is the antidote to our loneliness and isolation. Although we will have to take the risk that if people know us they may not like us, most of the time we will find that people actually like us *more* when we are honest, even about the things we don't want them to know. When we speak the truth about ourselves—when people know our story and love us anyway—we receive a gift we cannot obtain in any other way. The acceptance and love that we long for come only through truth telling: telling our story, listening to others tell their story, and giving honest feedback about our reactions.

This need for honesty in relationships is nothing new. Back in 1738, John Wesley, the founder of Methodism, drew up some guidelines for small groups. The Methodist Class Meeting, a small accountability group, was foundational to the denomination's practice of their faith. Although the way these guidelines are phrased may sound dated, notice how relevant they are for meaningful community even in our day:

> *The design of our meeting is, to obey that command of God, "Confess your faults one to another, and pray one for another, that ye may be healed." To this end, we intend . . .*

1. *To meet once a week, at the least.*
2. *To come punctually at the hour appointed, without some extraordinary reason.*
3. *To begin (those of us who are present) exactly at the hour, with singing or prayer.*
4. *To speak each of us in order, freely and plainly, the true state of our souls, with the faults we have committed in thought, word, or deed, and the temptations we have felt, since our last meeting.*
5. *To end every meeting with prayer, suited to the state of each person present.*
6. *To desire some person among us to speak his own state first, and then to ask the rest, in order, as many and as searching questions as may be, concerning their state, sins, and temptations.*

What if our small groups had such guidelines? Although it might not be easy for us to reveal "the true state of our souls, with the faults we have committed . . . and the temptations we have felt," it would surely draw us all into a rich kind of connection with each other! And that is really the only way to be rescued from the isolation that plagues so many of us.

Accountability works both ways. It requires us to be honest about our own struggles, but it also requires that we ask what Wesley called "searching questions" about the struggles of others. Our culture strives to be accepting and tolerant of almost anything, and it's hard for us to challenge one another or ask people to look at what is behind their behavior. But that's part of how God helps us to grow:

through the loving challenge of others. In that uncomfortable place, where we say words that are risky, we see God at work. We have the privilege of bringing God's truth to someone who needs it.

The ultimate goal of accountability is growth. It should never be used to shame, callously criticize, or be judgmental of others. It is an invitation for us to move toward God and leave behind whatever hinders us. It is an invitation for us to find the community and connection that our hearts long for. Indeed, that is why we were created in God's image: to have connection with him and connection with each other.

ACCOUNTABILITY AND TRUTH

PERSONAL STUDY: 2 John; 3 John; Jude
SCRIPTURE MEMORY: Ephesians 5:21
ON YOUR OWN: The Value of Transparency

"The church is a hospital for sinners, not a museum for saints."

—Pauline Phillips

"Don't hunt through the Church for a hypocrite. Go home and look in the mirror. Hypocrites? Yes. See that you make the number one less."

—Billy Sunday

When Cain asked, "Am I my brother's keeper?" (Genesis 4:9), his hostility and defensiveness were clearly evident. In our day, most people feel the same discomfort in trying to establish close, intimate connections with other people. If independence and self-reliance are the heroic traits of our day, then mutual self-disclosure and vulnerability tend to be avoided. Even if we believe there are advantages to nurturing in-depth relationships, we stay at arm's length because of fear and unfamiliarity.

In this study, we will build on the concepts of accountability to God and spiritual leaders (discussed previously) by exploring our accountability to each other. We will also examine how we are to speak the truth to one another and receive the truth from one another. The church can't be the church without this interaction.

Am I My Brother's Keeper?

1. *Read Romans 15:14.* What are the characteristics necessary for those who are "competent to instruct one another"?

2. *Turn to Galatians 5:25–6:2.* What do you think it means to "live by the Spirit" and be "in step with the Spirit"?

3. What practical advice for being accountable to one another can you find in these verses?

Four Practical Steps for Accountability

Chuck Swindoll made the following observation in his book *Living Above the Level of Mediocrity*: "Accountability includes opening one's life to a few carefully selected, trusted, loyal confidants who speak the truth—who have the right to examine, to question, to approve, and to give counsel." Here are four practical steps you can take to make yourself more accountable:

- Open up your life.
- Choose your confidants.
- Speak the truth.
- Grant the right to examine.

Open Up Your Life

4. What do you think opening your life would involve?

Choose Your Confidants

5. What strengths would a person need to possess before you would open up to him or her?

6. What would it take for you to establish a relationship like that?

Speak the Truth

7. What factors keep you from speaking the truth to others?

Grant the Right to Examine

8. What does it mean to give someone the right to examine your life?

9. Practically speaking, how would you go about choosing a person who would keep you accountable?

10. What kinds of help could your accountability partner provide?

Telling Each Other the Truth

Our modern society prominently displays a discouraging feature: lack of intimacy. Close, extended families seem to be a thing of the past. Even relatives who live close by often do not show the kind of trust and authenticity we long for in personal relationships. The burdens of heavy work schedules, outside activities, tending to children, and keeping up with everyday chores often intrude on the intimacy between husbands and wives. Friendships—because they frequently develop casually and without real purpose—end up being superficial and noncommittal. We are a society of people all alone with each other.

One of the deplorable effects of this situation is seen in how we try to talk to each other about what we see in each other. Our compliments often seem artificial and forced. If we try to offer helpful criticism, we tend toward opposite extremes: either we don't speak as honestly as we should (*polite people don't say such things*, we may think), or we blast one another with harsh judgments that relieve our pent-up feelings but do little to help the other person. God never intended the church to be so out of touch with itself. Next to the Scripture, God's chief mouthpiece for messages of encouragement or correction is our fellow believers.

This next exercise may be more difficult for some than for others, but don't get discouraged if you feel a little threatened by the thought of deeper honesty (positive and negative) with your fellow spiritual pilgrims. Learning to tell and receive truth is a goal for every disciple who wants to become like Jesus. This lesson will move you a step closer to that end.

Practicing Honesty

11. *Read Ephesians 4:15–16 and 4:25.* How would you interpret the phrases "speaking the truth in love" and "speak truthfully to your neighbor"?

12. Why is it so important for your spiritual well-being for the other people in your group to speak honestly with you?

13. What is the most difficult part of saying tough things to other people?

14. What makes it hard for you to say tender words to others?

Speaking the Truth in Love

The purpose of the rest of your group's time together is to give and receive personal feedback about each other. Observations can be either positive or negative, but your remarks should *always* stem from a desire to build up or help the person being observed. Positive comments should allow the person to recognize spiritual strengths that are a blessing to others. Praise should be sincere and not forced.

If you offer criticism, it should always be tempered by a concern for that person's well-being. Your observations are just that—observations, which are given from a limited but caring point of view. Here are some examples of how to state your observations:

- Mary, I have observed that you . . .
- Susan, one thing I really admire about you is . . .
- Dave, I'm concerned that you . . .

By phrasing your observations this way, you are admitting that you don't *know* for sure everything about a person's situation. You are saying you care enough to comment on what you see, and you readily admit the old adage is probably true: "If you spot it, you got it." Humility demands you to recognize your own similar faults and to realize there is always more to everyone's story than what you perceive.

By proceeding with a humble, encouraging spirit, our truth-loving heavenly Father can use your time together to create a powerful, life-changing event.

Apply It to Your Life

15. From this study, what would you say are the benefits of being held accountable?

16. What could you do this week to move in the direction of greater account-ability?

17. What could you do to better speak the truth in love?

Your Walk with God

Bible

Schedule three times this week to be alone with God. Each day, read the passage indicated below and answer the questions that follow.

DAY ONE: 2 JOHN 1–13

Some of the things I observe in this passage:

One idea for how to apply this passage to my life:

DAY TWO: 3 JOHN 1–14

Some of the things I observe in this passage:

One idea for how to apply this passage to my life:

DAY THREE: JUDE 1–25

Some of the things I observe in this passage:

One idea for how to apply this passage to my life:

Prayer

On each of your three days with God this week, pray for one area where you need help with accountability *and* for someone else who needs such help. Also pray for a different member of your group who is struggling with a problem that he or she brought up during the meeting.

Scripture Memory

Memorize this verse this week:

Submit to one another out of reverence for Christ (Ephesians 5:21).

On Your Own: The Value of Transparency

Pick up any tabloid or popular magazine and you will see stories of celebrities, politicians, or other leaders who are confessing to this or that lurid activity. Many television shows are based on a "reality" setting where cameras have access to people's private conversations and actions that most of us would never reveal to close friends—let alone millions of viewers on TV. And social media is often a place of sharing details that are really inappropriate for that setting.

So, in this culture of supposed "openness and honesty," how are we to live differently and bring honor to Christ without becoming voyeuristic? The answer lies in intention: *why* we are making ourselves vulnerable and transparent to each other and what is the *setting* for doing so. For most of the world, these kinds of disclosures are happening either for entertainment or for getting attention. The goal is not Christlike character; in fact, a lot of what passes for honesty and openness is really just a way to brag—and that to complete strangers.

Even if someone actually feels bad about their actions, their regret rarely translates into repentance. They are not saying, "I want to be a better person"; rather, they just want to get something off their chest, or own their "mistakes," or get sympathy. There is a woeful lack of intention to change. As one author and researcher noted, "Being vulnerable with a larger audience is only a good idea if the healing is tied to the sharing, not to the expectations I might have for the response I get."

For so many in the spotlight, it is all about the responses, not about healing. Also at play is the fact that for many in our culture, there are no moral right and wrongs; there are only preferences for some behaviors and aversion to others (which can vary from person to person). So people aren't trying to move from sin to holiness but are simply acknowledging that, though they previously got away with something, they've now been caught and now have to face the consequences. God's point of view, or moral right and wrong, isn't even in the picture. There's only what the person has to do to get back in favor with the one they love, or what they can do to regain the confidence of constituents they want to have vote for them again.

By contrast, let's revisit John Wesley's words from the last "On Your Own" section, where he talked about being vulnerable to one another in a small-group setting. Here is more from his rules for group members:

Some of the questions proposed to every one before he is admitted among us may be to this effect.

1. *Have you the forgiveness of your sins?*
2. *Have you peace with God, through our Lord Jesus Christ?*
3. *Have you the witness of God's Spirit with your spirit, that you are a child of God?*
4. *Is the love of God shed abroad in your heart?*
5. *Has no sin, inward or outward, dominion over you?*
6. *Do you desire to be told of your faults?*
7. *Do you desire to be told of all your faults, and that plain and home?*
8. *Do you desire that every one of us should tell you, from time to time, whatsoever is in his heart concerning you?*
9. *Consider! Do you desire we should tell you whatsoever we think, whatsoever we fear, whatsoever we hear, concerning you?*
10. *Do you desire that, in doing this, we should come as close as possible, that we should cut to the quick, and search your heart to the bottom?*
11. *Is it your desire and design to be on this, and all other occasions, entirely open, so as to speak everything that is in your heart without exception, without disguise, and without reserve?*

Any of the preceding questions may be asked as often as occasion requires; the four following at every meeting.

1. *What known sins have you committed since our last meeting?*
2. *What temptations have you met with?*
3. *How were you delivered?*
4. *What have you thought, said, or done, of which you doubt whether it be sin or not?*

First, note the setting itself for this kind of openness and vulnerability. It is a private meeting with others who care about us—a small group, not a reality TV show. And only a few are taken into confidence, not the masses.

Second, note there is a clear sense of wanting to grow and change, rather than just "air out dirty laundry." In the world around us, we hear only the admission of making a "mistake" or of doing something "regrettable." But Jesus tells us we've offended a holy God with sinful behavior and probably hurt people who are made in his image. He wants our *character* to change, not just our *behaviors*. He certainly won't be impressed by an "image management" approach; he wants us to become pure and holy in thought, word, and deed. It is for this purpose we practice disclosure and accountability.

James 5:16 says, "Confess your sins *[as sins]* to each other *[not for public consumption]* and pray for each other *[don't gossip]* so that you may be healed." That's a much better model for vulnerability than our world presents!

> *"Live-tweeting your bikini wax is not vulnerability. Nor is posting a blow-by-blow of your divorce. That's an attempt to hot-wire connection. But you can't cheat real connection. It's built up slowly. It's about trust and time."*
>
> —BRENÉ BROWN

LIFE-CHANGING COMMUNITY

This review culminates your study of Part 1, "Life-Changing Community." Use this time to reflect on your experience and summarize what you've learned about the church. This is also a time to appreciate and be grateful for what God has accomplished in you. This study will help you assess what you've learned and how you've grown.

Reflect on What You've Learned

1. Since we began, what discoveries have you made about yourself and your role in the church?

2. How has your view changed of what an "ideal" church is supposed to be?

3. In what ways can your own church be more like the church God wants?

4. In what ways can you contribute to the kind of change God wants to see in your church?

Self-Evaluation

Your group leader will be meeting with you to discuss your current spiritual condition and your hopes for growing in your faith. Please take some time to reflect honestly on where you stand right now within these four basic categories of Christian growth. Rate yourself in each category.

+ DOING WELL. I'M PLEASED WITH MY PROGRESS SO FAR.

X ON THE RIGHT TRACK, BUT I SEE DEFINITE AREAS FOR IMPROVEMENT.

− THIS IS A STRUGGLE. I NEED SOME HELP.

A Disciple Is One Who . . .

5. *Walks with God.* To what extent is my Bible study and prayer time adequate for helping me walk with God?

   Rating: _____

   Comments:

6. *Lives the Word.* To what extent is my mind filled with scriptural truths so that my actions and reactions show I am being transformed?

   Rating: _____

Comments:

7. *Contributes to the work.* To what extent am I actively participating in the church with my time, talents, and treasures?

    Rating: _____

    Comments:

8. *Impacts the world.* To what extent am I impacting my world with a Christian witness and influence?

    Rating: _____

    Comments:

9. Other issues I would like to discuss with my small-group leader:

PART 2

BUILDING YOUR CHURCH

What do you feel about the thought of being *used*? For many people, the term *used* is synonymous with *abused*. To be used means having someone else's agenda forced on you. It means being involved in an activity that you don't want to do, which leaves you feeling hollow and unfulfilled. It means giving to the point of exhaustion for the sake of something futile. If that's what it feels like to be "used by God," no wonder some of us can't get very excited about playing our part in the church!

But others see a different picture when they think of God using them. They see a caring heavenly Father who handcrafted them with special talents and abilities and longs for them to unfold according to his design. They know he created them with a plan in mind, and he wants them to flourish. They see themselves as givers as well as those who receive help. In serving, they experience more personal growth and greater impact than they'd ever dreamed—all because "God is using them." One can understand how such a vision would inspire these people to be involved in building their church for a lifetime.

One picture leaves us breathless with anticipation; the other, simply out of breath! So, how can we be sure we increase our service according to the right understanding? By understanding that God longs to give us living water for service—not so we feel *tapped out* but to help us feel *pumped up*. In our giving to others, he wants us to receive.

This section is designed to help you see how God made you and gifted you, not so he could merely "employ" you but so you'd experience the joy of being a co-builder of his eternal kingdom. That perspective can help you be a player in his work for the long haul. When your church is full of people with a similar under-standing, you will be a collective presence to be reckoned with. God will receive great glory.

And you will never be the same.

SERVING IN THE CHURCH

PERSONAL STUDY: 1 Corinthians 12
SCRIPTURE MEMORY: 1 Corinthians 14:1
ON YOUR OWN: Servanthood vs. Servitude

"Everybody can be great . . . because anybody can serve. You don't have to have a college degree to serve. You don't have to make your subject and verb agree to serve. You only need a heart full of grace. A soul generated by love."

—Martin Luther King Jr.

Attitude Is Everything

It's not enough to merely be an attender or even an official member of a local church. We need to be *involved*. Active service means being more than a spectator. God has accorded us the opportunity to be "players" by giving us spiritual gifts and material resources to make this contribution. Through our service, God fills us with a sense of accomplishment. When we contribute, we find fulfillment.

In this section, we will delve further into the ways in which we can contribute to the body of Christ. We will explore the following questions: *What should a believer's attitude be toward service? What are spiritual gifts? How do they help the church work in harmony for the benefit of all? How should Christians treat their material possessions? What part of a believer's income should go toward the work of the church?*

But before we move into a look at the spiritual gifts and the biblical teaching concerning our money and possessions, we need to affirm the *call to serve.*

Our Attitude toward Service

1. *Read Philippians 2:1–4.* How would you summarize the key thoughts in your own words?

2. What are some tangible ways we develop those attitudes in our lives? Be specific.

3. What prevents us from looking to the interests of others with the same attention we devote to ourselves (see verses 3–4)?

4. What does it mean that we are to have the same attitude as that of Jesus (see verses 1–2)?

Our Motive for Service

5. What should be our motivation for serving others (see verses 1–2)?

6. What could help you have more of the same attitude Christ had? Be specific.

7. What one word do you think best describes the attitude spoken of and modeled by Christ?

God's Call to Service

8. *Read Matthew 20:25–28.* How does Jesus challenge our customary ideas of how to attain greatness?

9. *Read Matthew 25:31–46.* In this parable of the sheep and goats, what is the main distinction between the two groups?

10. *Turn to Acts 2:42–47.* How did members of the early church serve each other?

11. How do people in the church today serve each other?

12. *Turn to Ephesians 2:10.* In what way are we God's workmanship?

13. *Read Colossians 3:23–24.* In what ways could we be serving Christ in our daily activities?

14. *Look at Hebrews 6:10–12.* Describe in your own words the benefit of diligent service.

15. *Now turn to 1 Peter 4:10.* For what purpose are we to use the gifts we have received?

Apply It to Your Life

16. What problem with or attitude toward serving would you like God to change in you?

Your Walk with God

Bible

Schedule three times this week to be alone with God. Each day, read the passage indicated below and answer the questions that follow.

DAY ONE: 1 CORINTHIANS 12:1–11

Some of the things I observe in this passage:

One idea for how to apply this passage to my life:

DAY TWO: 1 CORINTHIANS 12:12–20

Some of the things I observe in this passage:

One idea for how to apply this passage to my life:

Day Three: 1 Corinthians 12:21–31

Some of the things I observe in this passage:

One idea for how to apply this passage to my life:

Prayer

On each of your three days with God this week, pray for the following:

Day One: Think about how God has been patient with you and in what ways he has demonstrated faithfulness to you even when you were unfaithful toward him. Express your thankfulness to God for his kindness.

Day Two: Reflect back over the events, conversations, thoughts, and deeds of the past few days. For what do you need to claim God's forgiveness?

Day Three: Think of the material blessings for which you can thank God, and then read James 1:16–17. In light of your list, what is the significance of those verses?

Scripture Memory

Memorize this verse this week:

> *Follow the way of love and eagerly desire gifts of the Spirit*
> (1 Corinthians 14:1).

The next study will be the first of two on the topic of spiritual gifts. Before the next meeting, think of how you would describe a spiritual gift to a new believer. Also consider what gifts the individuals in your church possess that are particularly important to the well-being of the body.

On Your Own: Servanthood vs. Servitude

Most of us have some resistance to being labeled a *servant*. While it is true that in some circles the idea of servanthood has been held up as an ideal (for example, in business circles, "servant leadership" is mostly thought of as a good thing), the idea of serving someone else can often seem distasteful or even demeaning.

If you are part of an oppressed minority, servanthood might seem like slavery. Historically, slavery did exist in the United States, and talk of servanthood can trigger resentment or pain around that blight on our national legacy. Or it may be that you are part of a people group or minority that was—or is—being oppressed. For you, servanthood seems like passively accepting the injustice that was—or is still—being done. And it may be that because of your gender, social position, economic status, age, or even physical stature, others "expect" you to serve them. For you, the idea of servanthood is presumed upon you in a way that doesn't honor your dignity or humanity.

It's helpful at this point to look to Jesus and how he viewed servanthood. He held it in high regard, but only when it was not confused with servitude. The following is a list, with explanation, of important ways the two are different.

Servanthood Is Chosen; Servitude Is Forced

Jesus *chose* his servanthood status; he wasn't enslaved. At his baptism, the Voice from heaven reminded him that he was the beloved Son, in whom the Father was well pleased (see Mark 1:11). As the Son of God, Jesus knew he was powerful; but in his servant role, he kept his power at bay.

When Jesus was arrested in the garden of Gethsemane, he said that he could have called on his Father, who would have sent more than twelve legions of angels to do his bidding (see Matthew 26:53). But he chose not to use that authority so he could serve us by going to the cross. Even when Jesus taught that the greatest among us would be the servant of all (see Mark 9:35), the assumption was that we could choose to be that (or not).

Servitude is slavery, and nobody chooses that. If we think our only option is to obey, then we have no choice; consequently, we are not serving, we are complying. If we'd rather be doing something else but are forced to do an activity, we will most certainly view it as servitude. It's possible that the "we have to!" is self-imposed, but therein lies the difference. Whether by our own tyranny or the tyranny of another, if we *have* to, we're not *free* to. That's servitude, not servanthood.

Servanthood Supports Self-Esteem; Servitude Is Degrading

Jesus said there would be more blessing in giving than receiving (see Acts 20:35). In like manner, there is blessing when we serve rather than when we are served. Sometimes, we receive a grateful response for our acts of service, and that appreciation can build up our self-esteem. But even if we do not receive this response, as we serve we can know that what we are doing is worth doing, that it's a good thing we're doing it, and that we are a good person for choosing to do it.

Servitude makes us feel "less than," and those who enforce it on us send that message. Servitude leaves us feeling as if we shouldn't have to do this; sometimes what is required of us makes us feel dirty or used. We might do a task we judge to be beneath us as a servant, but if we feel bad about ourselves afterward, it is probably because we engaged in—or had an attitude that made it—servitude.

Servanthood Is Done by the Strong; Servitude Presumes Weakness

Only the strong can work hard for a good result. If we choose an action, by definition that requires us to be able to *not* choose it. Having a choice means we have power. We can choose to *throw ourselves* into an act of servanthood, but someone else *throws us* into a place of servitude. If we do the throwing we are powerful, but if someone does it to us, we are weak.

Servanthood Is Practiced by All; Servitude Maintains Control over Others

We can serve as followers, but we can also serve as leaders. In fact, leadership in the biblical sense requires an attitude of "doing for others" with a servant's heart. We can all think of people who serve with joy, whether as a follower or as a leader.

Servitude is a way for someone else to control us. If we lead that way, we exploit rather than serve, and the one exploited is not a servant but a slave. The only way a slave can lead is by exploiting in the same manner he or she is being exploited. When control is imposed, servanthood vanishes and is replaced by servitude.

Servanthood Produces Satisfaction; Servitude Creates Resentment

When we serve, we feel good about ourselves and what we've done. We know we had choices, and we're glad we made the choice to serve. We look at what we did and would do it again. We've done good work, and we are proud of it.

Servitude produces a sense of dissatisfaction. We don't like that we had to do it; we don't feel like we had a choice; we're not happy with the result; and we would not do it again if given the choice. We are not proud of what we've done. We're probably just glad it's over and we can move on to something else. We have no sense of being a better human beings. In fact, we probably think less of ourselves and maybe even feel ashamed.

Servanthood Always Does Good; Servitude Uses Others for Evil

To practice servanthood means a good result is forthcoming. We view it as a good person doing a good work. Others around us may not appreciate what has been accomplished, but if they stopped to notice, they would see that good was done.

Servitude is getting people to do evil things. People may have objections, but servitude negates those reactions and forces actions that violate people's consciences. If choice were allowed, people might choose to leave; servitude makes people feel as if they have to choose between two bad things. They know the consequences will be dire if they object, so they simply have to comply or suffer great personal harm.

Where to Go from Here?

You may want to go through the above list and think of various situations in which you are "serving," and then ask yourself whether it is servanthood or servitude. If you find yourself in the latter category, perhaps a change in attitude will help. But if not, it's probably time to move on so you can be a servant as Jesus envisioned— and not a slave to others, which Scripture teaches us to avoid (see Romans 8:15; 1 Corinthians 7:23).

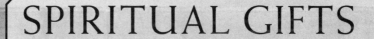

SPIRITUAL GIFTS

PERSONAL STUDY: Romans 12; 1 Corinthians 13
SCRIPTURE MEMORY: Ephesians 6:7;
1 Corinthians 12:7
ON YOUR OWN: Assessing Your Gifts

*"The gifts of the Spirit make us unique;
the fruit of the Spirit makes us one."*

—MIKE FRANS

What Are Spiritual Gifts?

The Holy Spirit has given every believer unique gifts that are to be used to accomplish God's purposes. Everyone can feel a part of the grand design when he or she employs these gifts in the way God intended. So, what's your gift?

Finding your niche can be as simple as understanding what the Bible says about gifts and then discovering and using those gifts in your church. It is exciting to learn that spiritual gifts are given to every Christian, but it's sobering to learn how greatly God depends on us to use our gifts wisely to accomplish his work. Still, many believers have only a murky understanding about spiritual gifts and how they relate to the work of the church.

In this study, you will learn more about how God intended spiritual gifts to work in the body of Christ. You will also be given a simple classification of gifts so you and your group can grasp how these are to be used in the church.

1. *Read 1 Corinthians 12:1–11.* What does Paul wish for believers regarding spiritual gifts (see verse 1)?

2. How do we decide what spiritual gift we will receive (see verses 4–6, 11)?

3. Why does God give us spiritual gifts (see verse 7)?

4. Why would the goal of spiritual maturity not be to obtain as many gifts as possible (see verses 28–30)?

5. *Turn to Ephesians 4:7–16.* How would you describe the kind of church that results when people discover and use their spiritual gifts?

6. What must be added to our gifts to make them beneficial to the giver and the recipient (see 1 Corinthians 13:1–3)? Why do you suppose that Paul had to include this instruction?

Primary Spiritual Gifts

Imagine a family with a permanent Christmas tree in their house. Under that tree sits a pile of presents—each one purchased with love and thoughtfulness and then carefully wrapped and put under the tree. Yet it would be a shame if the presents remained there, beautifully wrapped but never enjoyed as the packages of love they were intended to be. The receivers would never experience the gifts, the givers would never be appreciated for giving the gift, and the family would never benefit from the use of the gift.

Your church was not designed to be a house full of wrapped gifts. When all members know the gifts God has given them and use them for the common good, everybody wins—the receiver becomes fruitful and fulfilled, the body receives the ministry God intended, and God is glorified whenever the church operates according to his design.

One categorization of spiritual gifts divides them into two broad types: *primary* gifts and *complementary* gifts. The primary gifts can be further subdivided into speaking, service, and relational gifts. The chart on the next page shows this breakdown:

PRIMARY GIFTS	COMPLEMENTARY GIFTS	ADDITIONAL GIFTS
Speaking Gifts • Prophecy • Teaching *Service Gifts* • Administration • Helping • Giving *Relational Gifts* • Encouragement • Evangelism • Hospitality • Leadership • Mercy • Shepherding	• Apostleship • Discernment • Faith • Healing • Interpretation • Knowledge • Miracles • Tongues • Wisdom	• Craftsmanship • Creative Communication

Now that we have the big picture, let's look at the primary gifts in detail.

Speaking Gifts

7. According to 2 Corinthians 12:7–10, what potential problem could someone who has the *gift of prophecy* develop?

8. What is the warning of James 3:1 to those who have the *gift of teaching*?

9. What role do the speaking gifts play in the life of the church?

Service Gifts

10. Why was the *gift of administration* so vital to the ministry of the early church (see Acts 6:1–4)? Why is it still needed in churches today?

11. In Philippians 2:25–30, how did Epaphroditus exhibit the *gift of helping*?

12. What would you say are the differences between those who give to God's work (which is all of us) and those who have the *gift of giving*?

Relational Gifts

13. Why is the *gift of encouragement* so valuable in the church?

14. How would you describe the difference between the *gift of evangelism* and the responsibility all believers have for sharing the gospel?

15. In Acts 16:14–15, what can we learn from Lydia's *gift of hospitality* toward other Christians?

16. According to Hebrews 13:17, what are the main obligations of those with the *gift of leadership?*

17. In what ministries of the church would the *gift of mercy* be especially valuable?

18. Most people associate the *gift of shepherding* with the senior pastor of a church. But how might God use that gift in other ministries of the church?

Your Walk with God

Bible

Schedule three times this week to be alone with God. Each day, read the passage indicated below and answer the questions that follow.

DAY ONE: ROMANS 12:1–8

Some of the things I observe in this passage:

One idea for how to apply this passage to my life:

DAY TWO: ROMANS 12:9–21

Some of the things I observe in this passage:

One idea for how to apply this passage to my life:

DAY THREE: 1 CORINTHIANS 13:1–13

Some of the things I observe in this passage:

One idea for how to apply this passage to my life:

Prayer

On each of your three days with God this week, pray for the following:

Day One: Pray that God will grant you discernment in the days and weeks ahead to discover your gifts and use them in the most effective manner for serving the church.

Day Two: Reflect on the past week and think about any ways you have failed to demonstrate the love described in 1 Corinthians 13. Pray for three areas of character that you need God to strengthen.

Day Three: Think of people who have demonstrated genuine love in one form or another toward you and how that love was expressed. Thank God for them.

Scripture Memory

Memorize these verses this week:

> *Serve wholeheartedly, as if you were serving the Lord, not people* (Ephesians 6:7).

> *Now to each one the manifestation of the Spirit is given for the common good* (1 Corinthians 12:7).

The next study will examine the complementary gifts—those attributes that support and enhance the primary gifts. To prepare, think of a time when you played an important supporting role in someone else's work. What gifts did you bring to the job that contributed to the success of the effort? We will also examine ways of making sure you are working in a ministry that is suited to your particular gift.

On Your Own: Assessing Your Gifts

For next week's study, fill out the questionnaire below to help you identify your spiritual gifts.

Character Trait Assessment

This character trait assessment has been designed to assist you in identifying your primary gift(s). There are certain character qualities that often correspond to the manifestation of specific gifts in one's life. Place a check (√) by those statements that are true and best describe you or your tendencies most of the time. Total the number of items checked in each section.

SECTION A

____ You are more expressive/dominant than submissive/tolerant/inhibited.

____ You feel responsible to confront people with truth.

____ You tend to be strongly opinionated and individualistic.

____ You are able to apply biblical truths to everyday situations.

____ You are willing to experience brokenness to encourage brokenness in others.

____ Your messages bring conviction and change in the lives of others.

____ You tend to be more depressed than lighthearted about life and its problems.

____ **SECTION A TOTAL**

SECTION B

____ You are more composed/tolerant/empathetic than nervous/hostile.

____ You are willing to spend time caring/nurturing a group of people.

___ You desire and need intimate spiritual relationships.

___ You have a tendency to compromise rather than go to either extreme.

___ You are compelled to lead by example and model.

___ You spiritually develop others patiently and responsibly.

___ You are willing to renounce personal interests for the sake of others.

___ **SECTION B TOTAL**

Section C

___ You are thorough, careful, and skilled in details.

___ You are more composed than nervous, and more objective than subjective.

___ You are able to see the overall picture and anticipate possible implications.

___ You like to clarify goals and develop strategies to accomplish them.

___ You feel frustration and sadness when confronted with disorganization.

___ You are able to identify and effectively use resources to accomplish tasks.

___ You are concerned more for the productivity of kingdom work than personal desires.

___ **SECTION C TOTAL**

Section D

___ You like people and relate well to them.

___ You have a strong desire to share your faith with unbelievers.

___ You can discern spiritual needs in others.

___ You are more sympathetic/subjective than indifferent/objective.

___ You communicate the gospel with clarity, poise, and effectiveness.

___ You are committed to placing new converts in the body of Christ.

___ You enjoy building relationships with unchurched people.

___ **SECTION D TOTAL**

Section E

___ You are a conscientious person.

___ You prefer to give quietly without public notice, yet you need to feel liked.

____ You give gifts of enduring value.

____ You wrestle with being faithful in issues of money management.

____ You are able to give liberally and joyfully.

____ You desire to use your giving as a way to motivate others to give.

____ You feel a part of the work to which you give.

____ **SECTION E TOTAL**

SECTION F

____ You genuinely enjoy providing a place for others in need.

____ You appreciate every guest the Lord brings into your home.

____ You are concerned with meeting a need, not making an impression.

____ You tend to be easygoing and feel comfortable around strangers.

____ You are fulfilled by serving people who cannot pay you back.

____ You enjoy all classes of people and feel at ease with them.

____ You find that new people in the church migrate to you.

____ **SECTION F TOTAL**

SECTION G

____ Your friends seem to wait on your decisions.

____ You are able to motivate others toward a goal.

____ You consciously set an example for others.

____ You influence others to be all God wants them to be.

____ You are confident and practical and apply common sense.

____ You often feel alone in making certain decisions.

____ You are able to live with disagreement.

____ **SECTION G TOTAL**

SECTION H

____ You have a tendency toward a low self-image.

____ You find that others easily confide in you.

____ You have a strong desire to remove the causes of people's hurts.

___ You are empathetic, patient, tolerant, and impulsive.

___ You are able to express love in tangible ways.

___ You react harshly when people are hurt, displaced, or rejected.

___ You possess a positive faith that does not become easily depressed.

___ **SECTION H TOTAL**

SECTION I

___ You identify needs and desire to help meet them personally.

___ You are usually easygoing and loyal and want to be liked.

___ You enjoy serving when it frees others to better accomplish their ministry.

___ You are publicly more inhibited than expressive.

___ You have trouble saying no, which often results in over involvement.

___ You tend to feel inadequate and unqualified for spiritual leadership.

___ You like short-range projects better than long-range responsibilities.

___ **SECTION I TOTAL**

SECTION J

___ You study, understand, and share truth from God's Word.

___ You tend to be more objective/self-disciplined than subjective/spontaneous.

___ You like to gather truth and present it in an organized manner.

___ You listen with a discerning ear to the teaching of others.

___ You are analytical and make decisions based on facts.

___ You enjoy researching an idea and effectively communicating it to others at their level.

___ You are able to stimulate others to understand truth and obey it.

___ **SECTION J TOTAL**

SECTION K

___ You are more tolerant/sympathetic than hostile/indifferent.

___ You tend to be positive and full of faith.

___ You have a strong desire to see people fully mature spiritually.

___ You enjoy strengthening the weak and reassuring the unstable.

___ You view trials as divine opportunities for growth.

___ You like to challenge and are willing to rebuke to cause growth in others.

___ You spontaneously discern needs and individually encourage those in the trenches.

___ **SECTION K TOTAL**

Scoring

List, in order, the letters of the sections with the four highest scores (highest to lowest). Write in the corresponding gift.

SCORE	SECTION LETTER	GIFT
1	___	_____
2	___	_____
3	___	_____
4	___	_____

KEY

A. Prophecy   E. Giving   I. Helping

B. Shepherding   F. Hospitality   J. Teaching

C. Administration   G. Leadership   K. Encouragement

D. Evangelism   H. Mercy

DISCOVERING YOUR NICHE

PERSONAL STUDY: 2 Corinthians 5; Luke 16
SCRIPTURE MEMORY: 1 Peter 4:10
ON YOUR OWN: Spiritual Gifts Affirmation, Validation, and Checklist

"Here is the test to find whether your mission on Earth is finished: if you're alive, it isn't."

—RICHARD BACH

Complementary Spiritual Gifts

The church is many separate individuals but at the same time one body. Spiritual gifts help us work together with other believers so the church can function as one. Our gifts also distinguish us as valuable participants who can make a unique contribution to the life of the church.

Unfortunately, sometimes the gifts divide the body of Christ. People become proud of the gifts they possess and feel smug in their spiritual status. Others don't value some of the gifts and cut themselves off from the benefits that would come if everyone were allowed to make his or her contribution. Still others attribute undue importance to gifts that should be exercised in a support role. Paul wisely nestled the famous love chapter of 1 Corinthians 13 in the middle of his discussion on spiritual gifts so that we would be reminded of what the use of spiritual gifts is supposed to produce. With love as the goal, we can employ our gift and be "one" and "many" at the same time.

The last study covered the primary spiritual gifts: *prophecy, teaching, administration, helping, giving, encouragement, evangelism, hospitality, leadership, mercy,* and *shepherding.* Now we move on to the complementary gifts. These are so designated because they are intended to enhance the primary gifts. They do not function in isolation or assume the importance of a primary gift for either the individual or the church. In fact, problems can develop in a church when complementary gifts are elevated above the primary gifts. Complementary gifts serve best when they undergird and enhance the operation of other gifts.

This study will help you understand the purpose of the complementary gifts, determine how they should be exercised properly within the church, discover your own gifts, and learn how to find your niche.

1. What does a person with the *gift of apostleship* do (see Acts 1:23–26)? What problems might arise if someone tried to start a church without also having the gift of leadership and administration?

2. What is the difference between the faith we all possess and the *gift of faith* (see 1 Corinthians 12:9)?

3. In what ways might God give someone the *gift of healing* other than the sudden, dramatic gifts displayed by Peter (see Acts 3:6–7) and Paul (see Acts 28:8–9)?

4. What special instructions does Paul give in 1 Corinthians 14:11–12, 19, and 26–28 for the *gift of interpretation?*

5. Why is the *gift of knowledge* valuable for every church?

6. What special temptations or problems would a person entrusted with the *gift of miracles* face?

7. Why does Paul regard other gifts as more important than the *gift of tongues* (see 1 Corinthians 12:28; 14:2–5)?

8. How would you describe the difference between a person with the gift of knowledge and the *gift of wisdom?*

Additional Gifts

We can place any other spiritual gifts not specifically mentioned above in this category. People with these gifts also make valuable contributions to the body of Christ. (You may have other gifts you want to add to this list.)

9. How might the *gift of craftsmanship* be put to use in the church?

10. What is the value of having the *gift of creative communication* in the church?

Ministering in the Right Place

Does it make a difference which ministry you volunteer to do? Have you ever felt resentful because you were working in a ministry that you didn't particularly enjoy yet knew had to be done? Have you ever wondered what God is calling you to do?

Doing the right thing and having God's approval is important to ministry, but so is ministering in the right place. While many "soldiers of grace" are to be commended for diligently working without recognition and without reward, some people stay in the wrong place out of a misguided sense of duty.

People who are very involved in a church sometimes get the mistaken idea that the less they like their service, the more God must be pleased with it! In fact, God may have something better for them—a role more in keeping with their gifts, talents, and abilities. He teaches us in his Word that we all have different gifts so our uniqueness can be celebrated and our ministry can be both effective and personally fulfilling.

Discovering your gifts is the first step toward fulfilling God's plan for your life. Finding your particular niche is the next.

Identifying Your Gift

11. What is your primary gift? What other gifts or abilities have been affirmed by others who know you?

Developing Your Gift

12. Describe in your own words the principle that Jesus taught in Matthew 25:19–21. How might this idea be applied to spiritual gifts?

13. *Read Acts 18:24–28.* What do you see in this story about the development of spiritual gifts?

14. What are some ways you could develop your spiritual gifts? Be specific.

Misuse of Gifts

Notice the ways gifts—even though they come from God—can be misused:

- *Projection:* Expecting other Christians to possess our spiritual gifts and to serve as effectively as we do in similar situations.

- *Status seeking:* Holding our gifts as more important than other people's gifts and seeking special status for ourselves among other believers.

- *Isolation:* Using our spiritual gifts for personal satisfaction or gain rather than for the common good (see 1 Corinthians 12:7).

- *Suppression:* Suppressing the expression of our spiritual gifts because we doubt their validity, importance, or impact (see 1 Timothy 4:14).

- *Arrogance:* Taking credit for the results of our gifts instead of giving the glory to God (see Proverbs 25:14).

15. Which of the above abuses do you need to be alert to in particular?

16. Other hindrances can affect the fruitfulness of your ministry. As you look at the table below, what areas of weakness do you think could affect the use of your gift?

THE PRESENCE OF . . .	THE LACK OF . . .
Sin	Development
False Humility	Love
Pride	Availability

Gifts and Passions Assessment

17. In addition to spiritual gifts, we all have strong desires and interests that God uses to direct us into an area of service that fits us best. Take a few moments to answer the questions below relating to your passion or particular interest.

   - I prefer to work with:
     - ☐ Things   ☐ People
     - ☐ Information   ☐ Other _____

- I am attracted to and have the greatest concern for:

  ☐ Infants   ☐ Singles

  ☐ Children   ☐ Couples

  ☐ Teens   ☐ The elderly

  ☐ Young adults   ☐ Other _____

  ☐ Adults

- My deepest desire is to make a difference in the following area:

  ☐ Global concerns   ☐ Economics

  ☐ Politics   ☐ Other _____

  ☐ Secular society church

- I think the greatest need I could address is:

- If money, time, family, or education was not an issue, and if I knew I could not fail, I would do the following:

- If I could make a difference and impact an area of ministry, I would do the following:

- Based on my responses, the two areas that I have a passion for are:

Am I in the Right Place?

Sometimes a problem in the church occurs when people are willing to serve and are even faithful in their service but don't feel fruitful or fulfilled. If you're one of those people, you might be asking yourself, *Am I in the right place?*

18. In Acts 6:1–4, the twelve apostles realized they were performing tasks that weren't particularly suited to their gifts. What were some of the frustrations and problems developing in this situation? How did they solve the problem?

19. What steps could you take to determine if you are in the right ministry?

Your Walk with God

Bible

Schedule three times this week to be alone with God. Each day, read the passage indicated below and answer the questions that follow.

DAY ONE: 2 CORINTHIANS 5:1–21

Some of the things I observe in this passage:

One idea for how to apply this passage to my life:

DAY TWO: LUKE 16:1–15

Some of the things I observe in this passage:

One idea for how to apply this passage to my life:

DAY THREE: LUKE 16:16–31

Some of the things I observe in this passage:

One idea for how to apply this passage to my life:

Prayer

On each of your three days with God this week, pray for the following:

Day One: Pray for specific ways you can learn to live by faith, not sight (see 2 Corinthians 5:7), and make it your goal to please the Lord whatever your personal circumstances (see verse 9).

Day Two: Praise God for the gifts he has given you and the members of your group. Examine yourself and confess times when you've misused or neglected your spiritual gifts.

Day Three: Pray for each member of your group, asking God to develop each gift that person possesses for his service.

Scripture Memory

Memorize this verse this week:

> *Each of you should use whatever gift you have received to serve others, as faithful stewards of God's grace in its various forms* (1 Peter 4:10).

The next study will be the first of two on the topic of stewardship. To prepare, ask yourself, *How deeply does the pursuit of money control my life? What would it take for me to be more willing to give freely for the sake of others? What percentage of my income would I be willing to give away to advance God's work?*

On Your Own: Spiritual Gifts Affirmation, Validation, and Checklist

In the previous study, you completed an assessment to help you determine your spiritual gifts for *yourself.* For this activity, you will have two people who know you well complete an assessment to determine what gifts *they* see in you. Begin by following these instructions:

1. Make two copies of the Observation Assessment form found on the following pages.

2. Identify two people who know you well. Preferably, they should be Christians who have observed you in a ministry, or they should at least be people likely to have an accurate perception of you. (If you want more than two people to evaluate you, make additional copies of the assessments.)

3. Ask these people to read each gift description carefully and comment appropriately. Their thoughtful reflections will assist you in understanding who God made you to be. Ask them to return the assessment to you within one week.

4. Remember that people's perceptions will be affected by how long they have known you and the type of relationship they have with you (family, small group, work, and so on). Weigh these factors as you evaluate and record their responses.

5. Study the observations you receive, compare them against your own personal assessment, and determine which gifts seem to be most affirmed.

OBSERVATION ASSESSMENT FORM

Observations of _____

Completed by _____

Your friend or family member is seeking to better understand who God has made him or her to be. Your perspective and observations can be helpful in that process. Thank you for your time in completing this questionnaire.

Directions: Read each of the descriptions below. Using these definitions, mark one of the following letters in each of the spaces provided:

Y = YES, DEFINITELY TRUE, CERTAIN GIFT

P = PERHAPS, POSSIBLY TRUE, POTENTIAL GIFT

N = NO, DOES NOT HAVE THIS GIFT

? = I DON'T KNOW / I HAVE NOT OBSERVED THIS

____ **ADMINISTRATION:** The person understands what makes an organization function and has a special ability to plan and execute procedures that increase the church's organizational effectiveness.

____ **COUNSELING:** The person effectively listens to people and assists them in their quest for wholeness.

____ **CRAFTSMANSHIP:** The person facilitates ministry through the creative construction of necessary tools for ministry.

____ **CREATIVE COMMUNICATION:** The person has an ability to communicate God's truth through a variety of art forms.

____ **ENCOURAGEMENT:** The person reassures, strengthens, and affirms those who are discouraged or wavering in their faith.

____ **EVANGELISM:** The person effectively communicates the message of Christ to unbelievers so they can respond in faith and discipleship.

____ **GIVING:** The person contributes money and material resources to the work of the Lord with cheerfulness and generosity.

____ **HELPING:** The person accomplishes practical and necessary tasks that support the body of Christ.

____ **HOSPITALITY:** The person cares for people by providing fellowship, food, and shelter.

____ **LEADERSHIP:** The person instills vision in others, motivates them, and directs people to accomplish the work of the ministry.

____ **MERCY:** The person ministers cheerfully and appropriately to people who are suffering.

____ **PROPHECY:** The person proclaims God's truth with power and clarity in a timely and culturally sensitive fashion to correct, encourage, or lead others to repentance.

____ **SHEPHERDING:** The person guides, cares for, and nurtures individuals or groups in the body of Christ as they grow in their faith.

____ **TEACHING:** The person understands, clearly explains, and applies the Word of God to the lives of listeners.

Do you have any other observations or insights that would help this person to understand his or her strengths or abilities?

Look back at those gifts you marked **Y** (definitely true). List them from most apparent to least apparent, and then explain why you think this person has these gifts.

GIFT _____   WHY? _____

GIFT _____   WHY? _____

GIFT _____   WHY? _____

List in order the two top gifts you marked with a **P** (possibly true) and explain why you believe the person might have these gifts.

GIFT _____   WHY? _____

GIFT _____   WHY? _____

Spiritual Fit Checklist

The following checklist can be used to determine how well you fit with your current ministry involvement. Indicate your response to each of the five major areas by circling the appropriate number along each continuum below.

Does your ministry flow out of your **giftedness**?

- Do you have the spiritual gifts needed to fulfill your ministry responsibilities?
- Do your ministry responsibilities stretch your gifts to their fullest potential?

Not Suited   Perfectly Suited

1   2   3   4   5   6   7   8   9   10

Does your ministry reflect your **passion**?

- What need is of ultimate importance to you?
- Does your ministry in some way address this need?

Not Suited   Perfectly Suited

1   2   3   4   5   6   7   8   9   10

Are you receiving **relational affirmation**?

- Do your coworkers within the ministry verbally affirm your contribution?
- Does the leadership affirm you, or is there a curious silence from these people about your service?

Not Suited   Perfectly Suited

1   2   3   4   5   6   7   8   9   10

Are you receiving **ministry affirmation**?

- Are you being fruitful? Can you see results?
- Are those you are serving being encouraged and challenged?

Not Suited   Perfectly Suited

1   2   3   4   5   6   7   8   9   10

Are you receiving **personal affirmation**?

- Are you being fulfilled?
- Do you feel better about yourself after serving in this ministry? Is your self-esteem healthier?

Not Suited   Perfectly Suited

1   2   3   4   5   6   7   8   9   10

Scoring

Total the five numbers you circled:

45–50	You are serving properly.
38–44	You are probably in the right ministry, but you may need more experience serving.
30–37	You should make some minor changes in where you serve to make yourself more effective.
0–30	You should seek counsel with your church leaders regarding a ministry more in line with who God has made you to be.

MONEY MATTERS

PERSONAL STUDY: 1 Timothy 5:8; 1 Thessalonians 4:11–12; 1 Timothy 6:6–11, 17–19; Philippians 3
SCRIPTURE MEMORY: Luke 16:11; Hebrews 13:5
ON YOUR OWN: Can Christians Be Wealthy?

"Money never made a man happy yet, nor will it. The more a man has, the more he wants. Instead of filling a vacuum, it makes one."

—BENJAMIN FRANKLIN

"Wealth consists not in having great possessions, but in having few wants."

—EPICTETUS

Attitude Is Still Everything

The story of the rich young ruler is one of the saddest in the New Testament. Here we see someone who wanted to love God above everything, but money got in the way. Instead of repenting, he decided to walk away.

We may actually have more in common with the rich young man than we're comfortable in admitting. We may think we're open to Christ, impressed with who he is, and ready to respond to what he may demand of us. But when we find out what he demands of us and discover that he is Lord of everything—including our checkbooks and credit cards—our readiness may give way to regret. Our craving for righteousness may not be as strong as our appetite for money. The "things we are going to do for God" once our lives become manageable may, at the conclusion of our lifetime, end up being buried along with our overworked and prematurely deceased bodies!

The Rich Fool

1. *Read Luke 12:13–34.* What circumstance led Jesus to tell the parable about the rich man (see verses 13–15)?

2. What is the main point of the parable (see verses 16–21)?

The Rich Young Ruler

3. *Read Luke 18:18–30.* Which of the Ten Commandments had the rich young ruler failed to obey?

4. According to verse 27, how does Jesus respond to the question, "Who can be saved?"

5. What do you see as the main point of the passage?

The Shrewd Manager

6. *Read Luke 16:1–13.* What was the manager's plan to better his prospects after he left the rich man's employ (see verses 5–7)?

7. How do you understand the advice Jesus gave to the disciples about shrewdness and using wealth (see verses 8–9)?

Four Principles of Christian Stewardship

Bill Hybels of Willow Creek Community Church originally outlined the following four principles for Christian stewardship:

- Be faithful.
- Use money as a training ground.
- Ownership follows stewardship.
- Serve only one master.

8. *Be faithful*: What can you learn about faithfulness with finances from Luke 16:10?

9. *Use money as a training ground*: Why would handling money be a test for handling true riches (see verse 11)?

10. *Ownership follows stewardship*: Why is it important to be a good steward if you only have a little bit of money (see verse 12)?

11. *Serve only one master*: Why is personal financial management a true indicator of where your heart is toward God (see verse 13)?

What We Give

A tale is told of a man who was down and out, desperate, and had only two dollars left to his name. As he sat in church one day praying, he decided to place his last two dollars in the offering plate, believing that God would honor his faith and bless him in return.

As it turned out, the man walked out of church and immediately stumbled onto a business opportunity that required no initial investment and earned him a fortune within a matter of a few years. This same now-very-wealthy gentleman returned to the church where he had made his faith pledge. Before the sermon, he began to tell the man next to him about how he had sat in that very spot just a few years ago—in rags, crying out to God—and how he deposited his last two dollars in the offering plate.

"As a result," he related, "God made me a millionaire."

After a moment of reflection, the man sitting next to him responded, "You gave *all* the money you had to your name?"

The gentleman proudly replied, "That's right!"

The other man paused again for a moment, and then said, "I dare you to do it again!"

Generally, it's what we *keep* that exposes our attitude in giving. This is why the Scriptures emphasize motives and faith rather than dollar amounts and results. Certainly, carelessness and poor stewardship are as bad as stinginess and self-ishness. But we must examine ourselves under the light of God's Word, with the scrutiny of God's Spirit, to be sure that both how we give and what we keep is pleasing to God.

Principles of Stewardship

12. *Read 1 Timothy 5:8.* Why would a person who did not provide for his or her immediate family be regarded as worse than an unbeliever? What specific application could you draw from this verse?

13. *Turn to 1 Timothy 6:6–18.* How would you characterize the "great gain" Paul describes in verse 6?

14. How does Paul's advice to be content with food and clothing contrast to what our society tells us to be content with (see verse 8)?

15. Why is pursuing riches a trap? Why is it dangerous to love money (see verses 9–10)?

16. What advice does Paul give those who have wealth (see verses 17–18)?

Apply It to Your Life

17. What step could you take this week to put one of the principles of stewardship outlined in this lesson into action?

Your Walk with God

Bible

Schedule three times this week to be alone with God. Each day, read the passage indicated below and answer the questions that follow.

DAY ONE: 1 TIMOTHY 5:8; 1 THESSALONIANS 4:11–12

Some of the things I observe in these passages:

One idea for how to apply these passages to my life:

DAY TWO: 1 TIMOTHY 6:6–11, 17–19

Some of the things I observe in this passage:

One idea for how to apply this passage to my life:

DAY THREE: PHILIPPIANS 3:1–21

Some of the things I observe in this passage:

One idea for how to apply this passage to my life:

Prayer

On each of your three days with God this week, pray for the following:

Day One: Make a list of material wants that God in his grace has enabled you to taste and enjoy. Pray over your attitude toward money and the material things it can buy. What are you currently worrying about financially? What possessions (owned or yet to be obtained) are you serving?

Day Two: Pray for your use of money and that you may be faithful in giving in the quantity and quality God requires of you.

Day Three: Pray for those in your group who are struggling with their management of God's resources. Also pray for the financial stewardship of your church's funds and that the money would be spent wisely for God's work.

Scripture Memory

Memorize these verses this week:

"So if you have not been trustworthy in handling worldly wealth, who will trust you with true riches?" (Luke 16:11).

Keep your lives free from the love of money and be content with what you have, because God has said, "Never will I leave you; never will I forsake you" (Hebrews 13:5).

For next week, write a summary of the important points you gained from this lesson. Try to come up with five or six ideas. You will be sharing from these summaries next week.

On Your Own: Can Christians Be Wealthy?

Sometimes when we read about the great saints from church history, we might get the idea that truly committed Christians live very simple, even meager, lives. Often the impression is given—directly or indirectly—that riches are inherently bad and shouldn't be pursued. Even in our own day, whether from the pulpit where the evils of materialism are preached against, or from the world that is suspicious of Christians who have money, we get the general sense that poverty is somehow associated with godliness and devotion to Jesus.

Reasons such as the following are often given to promote the value of living free from material attachments:

- Jesus was poor by the world's standards. Shouldn't we be like him?
- Jesus said we cannot serve two masters, so it's either God or money.
- Money is the root of all evil, right?
- Many devout people down through the ages have taken a vow of poverty. Surely that means poverty is a preferred state.
- Riches produce worry, which Jesus condemns (see Matthew 6:25–34), and it is not a fruit of the Spirit (see Galatians 5:19–23).
- People with lots of money are often proud and arrogant.
- People with lots of money often look down on the poor and think they are that way because they are lazy.
- James says the rich oppress Christians (see James 2:6–7), so we should definitely not side with them or become one of them.
- Riches deceive people into complacency and keep them from trusting God.

The flip side of all this is a contrary teaching that encourages Christians to be wealthy. Some go so far as to suggest that wealth is a sign of God's favor. They also have a list of reasons for their point of view:

- Many people in the Bible (such as Abraham, Moses, King David, and King Solomon) were people of enormous wealth, and God's blessing was on them.

- God is wealthy—the whole universe is his!—so why shouldn't we be wealthy?
- The gospel brings good news to the poor, but doesn't say to *be* poor!
- Poverty is accompanied by poor health, disease, crime, and a host of societal problems. Christians should seek to *eliminate* poverty, not *encourage* it as a worthy lifestyle.
- The Christian way of living involves taking responsibility, working hard, clean living, not wasting money, saving, and other traits that naturally lead to becoming wealthy.
- We are to be generous and share. If we are poor, we cannot do that.
- We are "children of the King," and why would the King's kids be poor?
- John says he wishes for us to prosper *in all ways*, not just in our soul (see 3 John 2). It's a biblical promise we should claim.
- Blessings are often material as well as spiritual. If we shouldn't be spiritually poor, then we shouldn't be materially poor.

Somewhere in the middle of these two extremes we will find the right balance that takes into account the complex teaching the Bible offers on the subject. Let's go back through those lists of "reasons" and put them in proper perspective. We will begin with those who state that Christians should be poor.

- Yes, Jesus was poor. He was also single, but nobody claims that is a universal requirement for all Christians. He was also the only begotten Son of God, and we are not. We are to be like him in character, but not necessarily in all aspects of his lifestyle.
- It's true we should not have two masters, but that says nothing about how much money it would take for us to become a slave to it. Poor people can be just as obsessed with money as rich people. Jesus' concern about money is *mastery by*, not *possession of*.
- Money is *not* the root of all evil; the *love* of money is (see 1 Timothy 6:10).
- While there are benefits to a vow of poverty (and to a vow of celibacy), such vows are voluntary, based on God's prompting, and are not for everyone.

- Riches may produce worry, but so can poverty. The point is to avoid *worry*, not *wealth*.

- Pride is an inner condition that may or may not be linked to money. We are to work on our character rather than try to change external circumstances.

- How we view others may or may not be related to money. Looking down on others is not the exclusive domain of the wealthy.

- Not all rich people oppress Christians. Citing a specific historical situation and making it normative for all God's people, at all times, in all places, without taking into account the context, is not a proper way to apply Scripture.

- Riches *may* deceive people and make them complacent, but any person can lack trust in God regardless of his or her financial situation.

Next, to those who say we should all be rich, let's look at some balancing considerations:

- It is true that many people in the Bible *were* rich. They were also polygamists, adulterers, slave owners, and drunkards, but we don't suggest any of those traits should be the norm. God's blessing was on them *despite* many of the choices they made, not *because* of them.

- Yes, God is wealthy—and he gives it all away to us! Jesus was willing to set aside his wealth to live among us. Surely there is something there for us to consider!

- The gospel says that God loves us whether we are poor or rich. It commends neither wealth nor poverty, only that we live in connection with God.

- Poverty as a societal problem is one thing and is quite different from pursuing riches as the answer. We can work to eliminate poverty without suggesting Christians all have to be wealthy as the antidote.

- The Christian lifestyle *may* lead to becoming wealthy, but that isn't the goal. If the way we live does improve our financial condition, we are still obliged to share and be generous with our abundance.

- Poor people can be very generous, as evidenced by the story of the widow's offering (see Mark 12:41–44). Conversely, just because we have wealth doesn't mean we'll be willing to share it.

- Jesus *was* the King of Kings—and he was *poor*. There is no correlation between our identity in Christ and how much money we ought to have.
- Prospering is a good thing, to be sure; it's just not a guarantee. Nor should seeking prosperity be a primary goal above seeking *first* the kingdom of God (see Matthew 6:33).
- Blessings *are* often material as well as spiritual. But we are to be grateful for them, not demanding them or presuming that we should have them.

So where does that leave you? Your assignment is to reflect on the above statements (add some of your own if they are not on one of the lists) and write out your own summary of what you think God is telling you about what should be your attitude toward wealth. Compare your list with others in your group and see what learning you can share.

Remember that we all answer to God in these matters, not to each other. Use your brothers and sisters in Christ as guides, mentors, and counselors. But realize that you have only one Lord to whom you owe obedience.

GUIDELINES FOR GIVING

PERSONAL STUDY: 2 Corinthians 8:1–13; 9:1–14; Revelation 2–3

SCRIPTURE MEMORY: 2 Corinthians 9:7; Matthew 6:1

ON YOUR OWN: Giving in the New Covenant

"We make a living by what we get, but we make a life by what we give."

—WINSTON CHURCHILL

Perspectives on Stewardship

We all know the Bible gives us practical advice for living. All of us have turned to its pages for wisdom about family relationships, personal integrity, discipleship, and so on. But what does the Bible have to say about *money*? When we study the Scriptures, we find a rich lode of sensible advice for handling our financial affairs. From the book of Genesis through the letters to the New Testament churches, God has outlined a consistent, practical system for good stewardship. The purpose of this study is to expose you to the breadth of God's teaching on money and possessions and to help you apply that wisdom to your own circumstances.

1. What led you to choose the principles you ended up selecting from the last lesson?

2. *Read Philippians 3:8–9.* What enabled Paul to count everything as loss when compared to the greatness of knowing Christ?

3. How does James 2:14–16 speak to your present attitude regarding sharing with others?

4. What important principles of giving can be found from the meeting of Abram and Melchizedek in Genesis 14:14–20? What similar principles about giving do we find in Leviticus 27:30, 32?

5. What can we learn about the importance of the tithe from Malachi 3:8–10?

6. What did Jesus find lacking in the Pharisees' attitude toward tithing in Matthew 23:23? What principle about giving can we draw from Jesus' warning?

Guidelines on Stewardship

How does God look at the way we treat our possessions? An everyday comparison might be the way a parent observes and disciplines a young child. When the youngster is generous with his or her playmates—willing to share toys, a book, or snacks—the parent is pleased with the child's behavior. On the other hand, the child who refuses to share grieves the parent. In fact, such selfishness can anger the parent and might require some form of discipline.

God looks at our use of money in much the same way. When we give gladly and freely, it pleases him. But when we insist that everything we have is at our disposal and our discretion, it grieves the One who has given us everything we have. It is always his prerogative to bring corrective discipline to us if it would help. In this next section, we will look at what we should consider when giving. We'll look at the example of one New Testament church that struggled with the issue, and then we'll summarize the teaching on giving that we've learned so far.

Biblical Principles on Giving

7. *Turn to 2 Corinthians 8:1–9:15.* What do we know about the Macedonian churches that might encourage Christians who are reluctant to give because they have few resources?

8. What had apparently happened to the original commitment made by the Corinthians? What important principles of giving does Paul teach (see 8:6–15)?

9. What did Paul do to spur the Corinthians to action (see 8:16–9:5)?

10. What is a "cheerful" giver? Why is it important that we give "not reluctantly or under compulsion" (see 9:7)?

11. Why does Paul sum up his discussion on giving with an expression of thanks (see 9:15)?

Summary on Giving

12. Which of the following key principles from the New Testament is most difficult for you to accept? Why?
    - All that I have belongs to the Lord.
    - I should keep only what I need to meet my needs.
    - I should give the remainder to God's work.

13. What is the next step you should take to make this study a reality to you and your family?

Motives Matter

One day, while looking through the newspaper, you spot an ad that says, "OFFICE MANAGER WANTED. NO EXPERIENCE NECESSARY. GENEROUS SALARY AND BENEFITS. CALL 555–3331." You've been restless lately, hoping for a new challenge, so you decide to answer the ad. Surprisingly, you discover that no one else has responded to the notice. You go in for an interview and talk to a gruff old man who tells you that you'll be working for him. You're not sure you like him, but everything else seems satisfactory.

A few weeks into the job, you're unhappy. The work is repetitive and not too challenging, and the old man, while not rude, doesn't talk very much to you. You don't feel motivated to put in a full day's work, and you start cutting corners and taking longer breaks. But one day while your employer is away, you stumble across a file that contains some startling information. You find out that your boss is a multimillionaire. Moreover, you uncover a will that contains the names of past office managers—all of whom are slated to receive several hundred thousand dollars.

Overnight, you become the model employee. Your enthusiasm improves markedly, and your employer, noticing the change, compliments you on your renewed dedication. But in your mind you begin to hear nagging questions: *Am I just changing my behavior so I can get some reward? What are my motives for staying with this job? Am I being a hypocrite, only pretending to care about my boss's well-being when I really want his money?*

Christians should always subject their motives for serving others to the same kind of scrutiny. Jesus thought this was so important that he talked about it at length in the Sermon on the Mount. In this section, we will examine Matthew 6:1–18 and try to sort out the importance of motives in our service to God and others.

14. *Read Matthew 6:1–18.* Why would Jesus say a person who had publicly announced his deeds had received his reward in full (see verses 2, 5, 16)?

15. Why would motives matter so much to God? Isn't it sufficient to "get the good deed done" without examining motives?

16. What do you think causes people to have mixed motives when they serve? What tempts you to serve with mixed motives?

17. How can you have improper motives even when you pray (see verses 7–8) or fast (see verses 16–17)?

Your Walk with God

Bible

Schedule three times this week to be alone with God. Each day, read the passage indicated below and answer the questions that follow.

DAY ONE: 2 CORINTHIANS 8:1–13

Some of the things I observe in this passage (especially as they pertain to giving):

One idea for how to apply this passage to my life:

DAY TWO: 2 CORINTHIANS 9:1–14

Some of the things I observe in this passage (especially as they pertain to giving):

One idea for how to apply this passage to my life:

DAY THREE: REVELATION 2:1–3:22

Some of the things I observe in this passage (especially as they pertain to giving):

One idea for how to apply this passage to my life:

Prayer

On each of your three days with God this week, pray for the following:

Day One: Pray over the statement you selected as the most difficult principle in the New Testament on giving. Pray also for the needs of two other people in the group who have voiced concern about their giving and stewardship.

Day Two: Pray for yourself in regard to how you can be more of a contributing member of the church. Ask God to help you be a *relational* contributor, a *serving* contributor, and a *giving* contributor.

Day Three: Examine your motives for giving. Pray that you would give so that "your left hand [would not] know what your right hand is doing" (see Matthew 6:3).

Scripture Memory

Memorize these verses this week:

> *Each of you should give what you have decided in your heart to give, not reluctantly or under compulsion, for God loves a cheerful giver* (2 Corinthians 9:7).

> *"Be careful not to practice your righteousness in front of others to be seen by them. If you do, you will have no reward from your Father in heaven"* (Matthew 6:1).

In the next study, we will look at the seven churches described in Revelation 2:1–3:22. To prepare, consider what strengths and problems your church currently has. If Jesus were to return today, what would he find to praise or criticize in your fellowship? In what way, if any, is your participation in the life of your church lukewarm?

On Your Own: Giving in the New Covenant

By Dr. Gilbert Bilezikian, New Testament Scholar, Professor Emeritus at Wheaton College

It is generally recognized that, according to the Old Testament, the tenth of one's income represented a required minimum amount of giving to God's work by the people of the old covenant. The New Testament reverses this principle.

It requires new covenant believers to regard all of their income as belonging to God—not just the tithe (see Matthew 6:19–34; 19:16–30; Luke 9:23–25; 12:13–34; 16:1–13; 18:18–30; 21:1–4; Acts 2:44–45; 4:32–37).

The New Testament enjoins Christians to keep for themselves only that which is necessary to provide for them and their dependents so that they do not become a burden on others (see 1 Thessalonians 4:11–12; 1 Timothy 5:8; 6:6–10). Consequently, the portion of their wealth that exceeds what is necessary for their needs is to be used for God's work and for deeds of charity (see 2 Corinthians 9:6–15; Galatians 6:10; 1 Timothy 6:17–19; James 2:15–16; 1 John 3:16–18).

Thus, whereas the Old Testament required the contribution of only a tenth of one's income to God's work, the New Testament requires the total disposition of one's possessions for God, except the portion that is to be kept for oneself and one's relatives. On this basis, if the tenth of one's income is sufficient to provide for one's own and family needs, the remaining 90 percent belongs to God's work.

Old covenant believers were to set aside a tenth of their income for God. New covenant believers are to set aside for themselves only that which is required for their needs. The remainder belongs to God and is to be rendered to him as an expression of worship. This reversal of the old covenant standard provides an explanation for the New Testament's relative silence on the issue of tithing. The practical implications of the New Testament principle of total disposition renders the tithe obsolete, unless it is used as an aid to help Christians discover in greater fullness the joy of worship through giving.

For Christians whose limited income is only sufficient for subsistence, the tithe provides a goal to attain. For more affluent Christians whose income exceeds their needs, the tithe becomes restrictive. It is to be surpassed in the same measure that God prospers them.

To ensure the proper functioning of the ministries of the local church, it is appropriate for a body of believers to require that, apart from other giving, at least a tenth of their members' income be contributed to the local church that serves them. Both Old and New Testament offer warrant to uphold such a standard (see Leviticus 27:30–32; Matthew 23:23).

LESSONS FROM SEVEN CHURCHES

PERSONAL STUDY: Philippians 2
SCRIPTURE MEMORY: Hebrews 13:15–16
ON YOUR OWN: Church Priorities Worksheet

"The perfect church service would be one we were almost unaware of. Our attention would have been on God."

—C. S. Lewis

Letters from the Lord

Ephesus, Smyrna, Pergamum, Thyatira, Sardis, Philadelphia, and Laodicea. Are these exotic spices for a secret recipe? Or perhaps the latest in fashion colors?

In the book of Revelation, the apostle John was instructed by Christ to convey messages to seven churches. These churches often had both considerable strengths and serious shortcomings. Like our churches today, they struggled with losing their love for Christ and slipping into immorality, leniency, compromise, lifelessness, or casualness about their faith. The encouragement and warning that Christ gives these Christians is timeless, and all believers should heed these words as relevant to their own situations.

In this study, we will study the messages given to these churches. Pay special attention to the message to Ephesus, for its words of warning are applicable to many contemporary churches today. Also pay attention to Jesus' message to Laodicea, which had become lukewarm in its fervor for him and was ignorant of its spiritual poverty.

Ephesus

Ephesus was the capital of Asia Minor, a center of land and sea trade, and, along with Alexandria in Egypt and Antioch in Syria, one of the three most influential cities in the eastern part of the Roman Empire. The temple of Artemis, one of the ancient wonders of the world, was located in this city, and a major industry was the manufacture of images of this goddess (see Acts 19:23–41).

Over a long period of time, the church had steadfastly refused to tolerate sin among its members. This was not easy in a city noted for immoral sexual practices associated with the worship of the goddess Artemis. But many of the second-generation believers had lost their zeal for God. They were a busy church—the members did much to benefit themselves and the community—but they were acting out of the wrong motives.

1. *Read Revelation 2:1–7.* What commendable characteristics did the church of Ephesus possess (see verses 1–3)? How is your church commendable like the Ephesian church?

2. How had the Ephesian church fallen (see verses 4–5)? What did Jesus urge the Ephesians to do?

Smyrna

The city of Smyrna was located about twenty-five miles north of Ephesus. It was nicknamed the "Port of Asia" because it had an excellent harbor on the Aegean Sea. The church in this city struggled against two hostile forces: a Jewish population strongly opposed to Christianity and a non-Jewish population that was loyal to Rome and supported emperor worship. Persecution and suffering were inevitable in an environment like this.

3. *Read Revelation 2:9–11.* Why were the believers in Smyrna "rich" (verse 9)?

4. What were these believers about to suffer (see verse 10)? What reward did Jesus promise to those who withstood these trials (see verses 10–11)?

5. How would Jesus' words to this church be relevant to the situation your church is going through?

Pergamum

The city of Pergamum was built on a hill one thousand feet above the surrounding countryside, which created a natural fortress. It was a sophisticated city, a center of Greek culture and education, with a 200,000-volume library. But it was also the center of four cults and rivaled Ephesus in its worship of idols. The city's chief god was Aesculapius, whose symbol was a serpent, and who was considered the Greco-Roman god of medicine. It was not easy to be a Christian in Pergamum. Believers experienced great pressure to compromise or leave the faith.

6. *Read Revelation 2:12–17.* Why did Jesus praise the believers in Pergamum for their faith (see verses 12–13)?

7. What did Christ hold against the church of Pergamum (see verses 14–15)? In what ways might these ancient problems in Pergamum surface in your church?

Thyatira

Thyatira was a working person's town, with many trade guilds for cloth making, dyeing, and pottery. The city was basically secular and had no focus on any particular religion.

8. *Read Revelation 2:20–28.* What grievous sin had the church of Thyatira tolerated (see verses 20–22)?

9. What promise did Jesus hold out to those believers who had not stumbled (see verses 24–28)?

Sardis

The wealthy city of Sardis was actually in two locations. The older section of the city was on a mountain, and when its population outgrew the spot, a newer section was built below. The problem in the Sardis church was not heresy but spiritual death. In spite of its reputation for being active, Sardis was infested with sin. Its deeds were evil and its clothes were soiled.

10. *Read Revelation 3:1–3.* What kind of a reputation did the church of Sardis have (see verse 1)?

11. What did Christ urge the church of Sardis to do (see verses 2–3)?

Philadelphia

The citizens of Pergamum founded the city of Philadelphia. The community was built in a frontier area as a gateway to the central plateau of Asia Minor. Philadelphia's residents kept barbarians out of the region and brought in Greek culture and language. An earthquake destroyed the city in AD 17, and the aftershocks kept the people so worried that most of them lived outside the city limits.

12. *Read Revelation 3:8–10.* What difficulties did the church in Philadelphia encounter (see verses 8–9)?

13. What reward would the church of Philadelphia gain for its faithfulness (see verses 9–10)?

14. How do you think your church would respond to persecution? How would the rewards that Jesus promises be an encouragement to believers?

Laodicea

Laodicea was the wealthiest of the seven cities, known for its banking industry, manufacture of wool, and a medical school that produced an eye salve. But the city always had a problem with its water supply. At one time an aqueduct was built to bring water to the city from hot springs. But by the time the water reached the city, it was neither hot nor refreshingly cool—only lukewarm. The church shared similarities with Sardis, which had once possessed a reputation for fruitfulness but then slipped into decay. The church had become as bland as the tepid water that came into the city.

15. *Read Revelation 3:15–19.* What does it mean that the deeds of the Laodiceans were neither cold nor hot (see verse 15)?

16. Why did Jesus give this warning to the Laodiceans (see verses 18–19)?

17. In what ways could your church be considered a lukewarm church? In what ways could you be considered a lukewarm Christian?

Your Walk with God

Bible

Schedule three times this week to be alone with God. Each day, read the passage indicated below and answer the questions that follow.

DAY ONE: PHILIPPIANS 2:1–11

Some of the things I observe in this passage:

One idea for how to apply this passage to my life:

DAY TWO: PHILIPPIANS 2:12–18

Some of the things I observe in this passage:

One idea for how to apply this passage to my life:

DAY THREE: PHILIPPIANS 2:19–30

Some of the things I observe in this passage:

One idea for how to apply this passage to my life:

Prayer

On each of your three days with God this week, pray for the following:

Day One: Pray that your church would not lose its first love and that its work for the kingdom would be profitable.

Day Two: Pray that your church would keep itself from false teaching and immoral practices.

Day Three: Pray that your church would be ready for adversity and even persecution by standing up for Christ.

Scripture Memory

Memorize these verses this week:

Through Jesus, therefore, let us continually offer to God a sacrifice of praise—the fruit of lips that openly profess his name. And do not forget to do good and to share with others, for with such sacrifices God is pleased (Hebrews 13:15–16).

On Your Own: Church Priorities Worksheet

What is important to you when you look for a church? Once you commit to a church, what do you want to see happen in that church? What role do you want to play in its future? And what—if anything—would cause you to move on from one church to find a different one? Fill out the worksheet below to help you identify answers to those questions.

1. What I usually tend to notice about almost every church I visit is . . .

2. I think the top three indicators of a healthy church are . . .

3. If I saw any of these happening in a church I was visiting, I would probably not want to make it my home church . . .

4. What I look for in the teaching of a church I'm considering joining is . . .

5. What I look for in the people who are part of a church I'm considering joining is . . .

6. I most want to contribute to a church by being involved in . . .

7. I feel that a church needs to be always growing in these areas to assure me it's on track . . .

8. Some good reasons to leave a church are . . .

9. Some bad reasons to leave a church are . . .

10. If I see something wrong in my church, the best way to help without succumbing to gossip or being judgmental is . . .

11. While I expect to be disappointed in my church at some point (it's made up of people, after all!), if any of these things happened, it would make me seriously consider leaving . . .

12. The attitudes I might have and actions I might do that could cause harm to my church are . . .

BUILDING YOUR CHURCH

Training camp is over! It's time for the season to begin. In Part 2 you've learned, prayed about, and studied God's instructions for service. Now you've been placed in the starting lineup, and you will need to draw on all the resources you have available to put forth the best effort for God's team. He has called you, equipped you, and empowered you to carry out his will and build his church. Let's get our final instructions and then PLAY BALL!

Reflect on What You've Learned

1. What mistaken attitudes can you have in your service to God?

2. What prevents the church from exercising its spiritual gifts in an efficient, harmonious manner?

3. What are your primary spiritual gifts? In what ways can your gifts be best used to build your church?

4. Why are the complementary gifts to be used only to supplement the primary gifts?

5. If you were to try to convince a brand-new believer of the importance of discovering and using his or her spiritual gifts, what would you tell that person?

6. How would you summarize Jesus' teaching on money and possessions?

7. If you were asked by that same new believer to explain how God wants him or her to handle money, including giving to ministry, what would you tell that person? Write down at least three suggestions.

8. How will you handle your own resources differently as a result of this study? Be specific.

9. What passages of Scripture in this study have helped you rethink your attitudes toward possessions?

10. What principle should believers keep in mind when they're determining how much to give to their church or other ministries?

11. Looking back at the messages given to each of the seven churches in Revelation 2 and 3, what related problems in your own church did you find that could weaken its effectiveness?

12. What step could you take as an individual in response to Jesus' message to the seven churches?

Self-Evaluation

Your group leader will be meeting with you to discuss your current spiritual condition and your hopes for growing in your faith. Please take some time to reflect honestly on where you stand right now within these four basic categories of Christian growth. Rate yourself in each category.

+ DOING WELL. I'M PLEASED WITH MY PROGRESS SO FAR.

X ON THE RIGHT TRACK, BUT I SEE DEFINITE AREAS FOR IMPROVEMENT.

− THIS IS A STRUGGLE. I NEED SOME HELP.

A Disciple Is One Who . . .

13. *Walks with God.* To what extent is my Bible study and prayer time adequate for helping me walk with God?

    Rating: _____

    Comments:

14. *Lives the Word.* To what extent is my mind filled with scriptural truths so that my actions and reactions show I am being transformed?

    Rating: _____

    Comments:

15. *Contributes to the work.* To what extent am I actively participating in the church with my time, talents, and treasures?

    Rating: _____

    Comments:

16. *Impacts the world.* To what extent am I impacting my world with a Christian witness and influence?

    Rating: _____

Comments:

17. Other issues I would like to discuss with my small-group leader:

PART 3

MAKING A DIFFERENCE IN YOUR WORLD

The danger for any maturing disciple is that of becoming a *thermometer* instead of a *thermostat*. Immature believers *reflect* the temperature of the world around them, while disciples *set* it. The lifestyle of Jesus demands that we influence others as "salt and light" in the world. We can't be both salty and bland at the same time. We can't both shine the light and be dull. We can't be disciples without exerting an influence for Christ at home, at work, and among friends. In the end, we must *impact our world* through evangelism.

When people think of evangelism, they usually think of proclaiming a message. Depending on how they see themselves as public speakers, they will rate themselves as good or bad evangelists. However, there are many ways we can be evangelists to the people in our world, and not all of them require great skill at public speaking. What is required is an *understanding of the message*. To this end, in Part 3 of this book, we will focus on getting a handle on the content of the gospel. The combination of content and good illustrations can go a long way toward helping us to be more confident and thus more fruitful at personal evangelism.

Yet knowing the content is only a part of the package. Another key component is our individual styles. Depending on how God made us, there are many different approaches we can take when sharing our faith. Jesus used many styles, as did Paul and the other apostles. In addition to getting a clear grasp of the content of the gospel, then, it is helpful to discover our own style of presenting it. Merely discovering our style can free us from loads of guilt and frustration that may arise from trying to use styles with which we aren't gifted.

Still, New Testament evangelism is more than content and style. Paul described it this way: "Our gospel came to you not simply with words but also with power, with the Holy Spirit and deep conviction" (1 Thessalonians 1:5). The power and conviction of the speaker, along with the ministry of the Holy Spirit, make evangelism effective. In the end, it's that nonverbal component—that strength of person accompanying the message—that creates the life-changing impact.

This final section will help you and your group members *clarify* the message and *identify* styles—and challenge you to become players in God's kingdom. You'll see evangelism in its proper perspective: the natural result of a disciple's lifestyle. As such, you will truly become a person of influence, committed to imitating the ministry of Jesus. You and others who follow this same path will be the ones remembered for your fruitfulness. You will be the ones *impacting your world*.

EVANGELISM

PERSONAL STUDY: Acts 26; John 4:1–26, 39–54
SCRIPTURE MEMORY: Romans 3:23; 1 Peter 3:15
ON YOUR OWN: Personal Evangelism Worksheet

"Twenty years from now, you will be more disappointed by the things you didn't do than by the ones you did do."

—MARK TWAIN

Introduction to Evangelism

This will be a study about making a positive change in the people around you by helping them discover how to begin a personal relationship with Christ. In this study, you will explore a variety of ways to do personal evangelism and learn some practical tools that can help you feel confident and natural about your evangelistic efforts.

But before you begin to share God's good news with others, you first need to look at how *you* regard personal evangelism. Do you see it as a great privilege that flows naturally from your relationship with Christ? Or is it a touchy, awkward situation that you avoid unless it's forced on you? Many Christians are uneasy about this role to which they have been called and shy away from evangelism. In many cases, this reluctance results from a lack of true understanding of what is involved in sharing the gospel with others.

In this study, your will examine your preconceptions of evangelism, look at how the apostles in the early church shared the gospel with others, and consider some common misconceptions about evangelism.

Your Impressions of Evangelism

1. The feeling that goes through me whenever I am challenged to do personal evangelism is:

2. Up to this point in time, others have responded to my attempts at personal evangelism by:

3. My most memorable experience of being witnessed to by another person was:

Evangelism in the Early Church

4. *Read Acts 3:1–26.* In what way could you call healing the beggar an act of evangelism (see verses 1–10)?

5. What elements of effective evangelism can you find in Peter's speech to the crowd (see verses 11–26)?

6. *Turn to Acts 4:1–37.* How did Peter and John respond to the hostility shown to their message (see verses 1–12)?

7. How would you react if you had to defend your faith before a hostile audience?

8. How did the lifestyles of the new Christians support their evangelistic work (see verses 32–37)?

9. What steps could you take to see that your lifestyle provides opportunities for people to hear about Christ?

Me, an Evangelist?

What do you think of when you hear the word *evangelist*? For many, the term brings up all sorts of unpleasant images: hellfire-and-brimstone Bible thumpers; pushy-salesman types; slick, insincere celebrities; money-grubbing televangelists; bizarre cult-like figures; hustlers; con artists; and so on. And though our lives may not resemble the ones exhibited by these questionable figures, we may unwittingly fall into the trap of not sharing our faith with others for fear of being identified with these disreputable types.

But how do we fulfill the command to share the gospel without offending others? And how can we evangelize without making ourselves and our faith seem foolish? We'll try to confront these fears next by looking at some misconceptions regarding evangelism. We'll also look at an evangelistic tool called the "Impact List" that will demonstrate a straightforward way of reaching friends, coworkers, and family members with the gospel.

Misconceptions about Evangelism

10. What is it about the stereotypical negative evangelistic approaches that people find so objectionable?

11. What positive connotations do you have of the terms *evangelist* and *evangelism*?

12. Why might a positive regard for the work of evangelists actually diminish your own activity to win others to Christ?

13. In what circumstances might an "average" Christian have a more effective evangelistic ministry than someone who is more polished?

14. Matthew 5:14–16 and Romans 10:17 illustrate two distinct but necessary components to evangelism. How would you describe them in your own words?

15. How does 1 Peter 3:15–16 summarize these two components of evangelism?

The Impact List

In the table at the top of the next page, list the names of three people you know who need to hear about Christ.

In the second column, write down areas of common ground that you share with these people. In the third column, write down some practical steps you can take based on your areas of common ground to begin opening doors of communication with them.

NAME	AREAS OF COMMON GROUND	PLAN OF ACTION
1.		
2.		
3.		

16. How can you avoid giving the people on your list the impression that they are your "evangelistic project"?

Your Walk with God

Bible

Schedule three times this week to be alone with God. Each day, read the passage indicated below and answer the questions that follow.

DAY ONE: ACTS 26:1–32

Some of the things I observe in this passage (especially as they relate to evangelism):

One idea for how to apply this passage to my life:

DAY TWO: JOHN 4:1–26

Some of the things I observe in this passage (especially as they relate to evangelism):

One idea for how to apply this passage to my life:

DAY THREE: JOHN 4:39–54

Some of the things I observe in this passage (especially as they relate to evangelism):

One idea for how to apply this passage to my life:

Prayer

On each of your three days with God this week, pray for a person you've included on your Impact List. Ask God to help you be effective in your efforts to evangelize that person.

Scripture Memory

Memorize these verses this week:

For all have sinned and fall short of the glory of God (Romans 3:23).

But in your hearts revere Christ as Lord. Always be prepared to give an answer to everyone who asks you to give the reason for the hope that you have (1 Peter 3:15).

On Your Own: Personal Evangelism Worksheet

During the next meeting, you will consider the costs and benefits of personal evangelism and take a look at different styles of evangelism. To prepare for the study, go through the following worksheet and jot down your thoughts. This worksheet will explore the following topics: (1) ways that active involvement in evangelism can be of benefit to Christians; (2) why people don't want to be involved in evangelism; and (3) the distinctive aspects of your personality that would impact the way you share the gospel with others.

1. Although I share my faith to help others come to know God, doing that also helps me in the following ways . . .

2. It will challenge my own learning about the truths of Christianity if I have to explain . . .

3. I notice that when I think of sharing my faith, I feel some hesitation because . . .

4. What intimidates me most when I try to tell people about Christ is . . .

5. The main thing I need to learn if I am going to become more effective at evangelism is . . .

6. I think my personality gets in the way of sharing my faith because . . .

7. The most natural way for me to share Christ with others is . . .

8. I have enjoyed being part of spiritual conversations when . . .

9. What would make sharing the gospel easier for me is . . .

WHAT'S YOUR STYLE?

PERSONAL STUDY: Acts 8:26–40; John 3:1–21
SCRIPTURE MEMORY: Romans 6:23
ON YOUR OWN: Telling Your Story

"Many believers search their hearts . . . looking for the arrival of some feeling of benevolence that will propel them into bold evangelism. It will never happen. . . . Don't wait for a feeling or love in order to share Christ with a stranger. You already love your heavenly Father, and you know that this stranger is created by Him, but separated from Him, so take those first steps in evangelism because you love God."

—JOHN PIPER

The Benefits—and Cost—of Evangelism

When people decide to do something, the energy they expend is usually in direct proportion to the "WIIFM factor"—*What's In It For Me*. If people do not perceive any benefit in attempting an activity or plan, they are not likely to pursue it with much enthusiasm or energy.

Unfortunately, the WIIFM factor plays a decisive role in the evangelistic efforts of many Christians. They see considerable cost in sharing their faith with non-believers. They may think it is the right and even necessary thing to do, but they find it difficult to believe the discomfort or vulnerability they experience could have any benefit—unless the person responds to the message. But the chances of that happening, in their estimation, are pretty remote.

Such attitudes need to be reexamined in the light of Scripture. This study will demonstrate there are many benefits to be gained through personal evangelism. Yes, there are also costs, but they are far outweighed by the gains. You will also examine your own particular style of evangelism and how you can be the most effective in sharing the gospel of Christ with others.

The Benefits to You

- Joy
- Growth
- Confidence

1. **Joy.** *Read 1 Thessalonians 2:13, 19–20.* What can you infer about the personal satisfaction Paul derived from his ministry with the Thessalonians?

2. **Growth.** *Read Acts 9:19–22.* What was the message that Paul (called Saul here) preached after his conversion? What evidence of spiritual growth do you see from the description of Paul in verse 22?

3. **Confidence.** *Turn to Romans 1:16.* How would you describe Paul's respect for the gospel?

The Benefits to Others

- Salvation
- Life to the full
- A new family

4. What do you think Jesus meant when he promised life "to the full" to those who believed (see John 10:10)?

5. How has being "brought near" to God's people been a rich experience to you (see Ephesians 2:13)?

The Benefits to God

- His glory
- His joy

6. How does God respond when a lost sinner finds salvation (see Luke 15:7, 10)?

The Cost of Evangelism

- Time and effort
- Potential rejection

 7. What encouragement did Jesus offer those who suffered rejection for his sake (see Matthew 5:11–12; 2 Timothy 3:12)?

Finding Your Evangelism Style

What kind of car do you drive? If you have a large family, you may own an SUV or a minivan. If you're single and just starting out, a compact car may be more along your lines. If you're involved in construction work, a pickup truck may be the best investment for you. When it comes right down to it, you probably chose your vehicle based on your personality and needs.

In the same way, you need to choose a style of evangelism that both fits you and helps you get the job done. Some people can win others to Christ with a direct, confrontational method. Others feel more comfortable arguing the reasonableness of Christianity in an intellectual manner. Still others find testimonials to be a winning formula. But whatever style you find appealing, it is vital that you put your preference into practice!

A Variety of Evangelistic Styles

- Confrontational
- Intellectual
- Testimonial

- Relational
- Invitational
- Service-oriented

8. **Confrontational.** *Read Acts 2:37–40.* What evidence can you find that Peter's bold style of evangelism had measurable results? Who in your group came to Christ as a result of being confronted with a testimony of God's power? How did it happen?

9. **Intellectual.** *Read Acts 17:16–34.* Why did Paul present a reasoned defense of the faith to the Athenians? Who in your group came to Christ as a result of reasoning and questioning? How did it happen?

10. **Testimonial.** *Read John 9:13–34.* What made the testimony of the blind man before the Pharisees so effective? Who in your group came to Christ as a result of hearing a powerful message of personal transformation? How did it happen?

11. **Relational.** *Read Mark 5:18–20.* Why did Jesus send the man who had been released from demons home to his family? Who in your group came to Christ through watching the change Jesus made over time in a close friend or family member? How did it happen?

12. **Invitational.** *Read John 4:1–30, 39–42.* How would you characterize the style of evangelism Jesus demonstrated to the woman at the well? Who in your group came to Christ through someone inviting that person to consider him? How did it happen?

13. **Service-oriented.** *Read Acts 9:36–42.* How did Tabitha demonstrate effective evangelism for the poor of Joppa? Who in your group came to Christ through someone's sacrificial service in his name? How did it happen?

Ways to Begin a Spiritual Conversation

- Direct approach
- Conversational bridges
- Invitation to an event

14. What kind of questions might you ask to begin a discussion on spiritual matters?

15. How might you steer a conversation on a general topic to a discussion about your faith?

Getting Ready to Tell Your Story

16. *Read Acts 26:4–23.* Why did Paul feel compelled to share the details of his life before his conversion (see verses 4–11)?

17. Why did Paul include the details of his conversion in his testimony (see verses 12–18)?

18. How did Paul describe the purpose of his mission (see verses 19–23)?

Your Walk with God

Bible

Schedule three times this week to be alone with God. Each day, read the passage indicated below and answer the questions that follow.

DAY ONE: ACTS 8:26–40

Some of the things I observe in this passage (especially as they apply to evangelism):

One idea for how to apply this passage to my life:

DAY TWO: JOHN 3:1–8

Some of the things I observe in this passage (especially as they apply to evangelism):

One idea for how to apply this passage to my life:

DAY THREE: JOHN 3:9–21

Some of the things I observe in this passage (especially as they apply to evangelism):

One idea for how to apply this passage to my life:

Prayer

On each of your three days with God this week, pray for the following:

Day One: Say a prayer of thanksgiving for new Christians in your church who have entered the kingdom because someone cared enough to explain Jesus' love for them.

Day Two: Confess any times when you have let opportunities for personal evangelism slip away because of fear or selfishness.

Day Three: Pray for the efforts of group members as they share the gospel with the people on their Impact Lists.

Scripture Memory

Memorize this verse this week:

> *For the wages of sin is death, but the gift of God is eternal life in Christ Jesus our Lord* (Romans 6:23).

Next time, you will take some time to practice telling others your own story. To prepare for the session, complete the assignment that follows.

On Your Own: Telling Your Story

For next week, fill out the worksheet below. When it's completed, go back and write out your story in three main paragraphs that correspond to the outline Paul used in Acts 26:1–23. You should be able to read your paragraphs in four to five minutes total.

Tips on Writing Your Story

- Make it personal—it's your story.
- Identify a theme that carries through all three paragraphs.
- Use ordinary language, not spiritual clichés. Ask yourself, *Would a non-Christian I work with understand what I am saying?*

■ Don't try to be sensational. It's not only dishonest (since you are exaggerating), but you will also fail to relate to ordinary people in ordinary circumstances.

Elements of Your Story

The following questions are meant to help you form ideas for your testimony. When you write out your full testimony later, you'll be able to expand on these abbreviated responses. (**Note:** If you received Christ when you were a young child, start with the third question.)

1. What was your spiritual viewpoint before receiving Christ?

2. Before you met Christ, how did your spiritual state negatively affect your life and relationships? Use specific examples.

3. How did you hear or learn of the gospel message that changed your life?

4. What was it about the message that affected you?

5. What was your response to that message?

6. When did you receive Christ?

(**Note:** Once again, if you became a Christian as a child, the emphasis on the next two questions should be on the benefits Christ has made in your life as compared to what it might have been like without knowing him, or to those times when you haven't been close to him.)

7. How did your attitudes and life change after you received Christ? (You should show that the problem mentioned in the second question was resolved.)

8. What other benefits have you realized since receiving Christ? Again, be specific.

9. With what problems do you still struggle? How is God helping to make a difference?

TELLING YOUR STORY

PERSONAL STUDY: Ephesians 2:1–10
SCRIPTURE MEMORY: 1 Peter 3:18
ON YOUR OWN: Reflections on the Essential Message of Christianity

"Introverted seekers need introverted evangelists . . . introverted seekers need to know and see that it's possible to lead the Christian life as themselves. It's imperative for them to understand that becoming a Christian is not tantamount with becoming an extrovert."

—ADAM S. McHUGH

Polishing Your Story

Have you ever given a public speech? If you have, you know what a nerve-racking event it can be. With so many eyes on you, it's important that you have your thoughts together. That's why preparation is so important.

By spending time organizing your points, writing out your statements, and rehearsing your delivery, you can produce a speech that your audience will enjoy and respond to favorably. If, on the other hand, you decide to "wing it," the results can be disappointing. You may stumble at critical points or drone on and on, losing whatever interest the audience may have had in your subject.

In this study, you will have an opportunity to do some polishing of the personal story you prepared for this week. Your fellow group members will be giving you input as to how your story can be made even more effective for the people you want to reach. And as you listen to other members' testimonies, you will also offer them constructive, beneficial comments. You will begin by discussing the following practical suggestions for sharing a testimony.

The Earlier the Better

1. Why is it important to share your testimony early in your relationship with somebody?

2. With whom on your Impact List have you not followed this suggestion?

3. How might you overcome your reluctance to share Christ with a person you feel may not be receptive to the message?

Give the Message in Doses

4. What problem do you see with meeting a person, sharing the gospel, and expecting a decision for Christ all at once?

5. What benefits can you see with giving the message in "doses" over time?

6. How does this approach allow you to build a better relationship with the person?

Share One to One

7. What advantages does one-on-one interaction have when sharing the gospel as compared to talking to a group of people?

8. What does sharing one-on-one in this manner communicate to the other person?

9. How can you get one-on-one interaction time with the people on your Impact List?

Be Transparent

10. Why is it important to let your feelings and personality show when sharing the gospel with others?

11. What are some ways you can demonstrate transparency with the people on your Impact List?

Sharing Your Story with Others

In this section of the study, you will read the story you prepared for this week to at least one other person in the group. The listener should then comment on your story, and then you will listen and comment as that person reads his or her story to you. Obviously, no one should discourage another member—the feedback should be positive. Any criticisms should be limited to fine-tuning the effectiveness of the story. When you are finished, discuss the following:

Sharing Your Own Story

12. What did you learn from telling your own story?

13. What positive feedback did you receive to help you know the strengths of your story?

14. What constructive criticism did you receive to help you improve your story?

Listening to Another Person's Story

15. What did you learn from listening to the story from the other person?

16. What positive feedback did you provide to help that person know the strengths of his or her story?

17. What constructive criticism did you provide to help the person improve his or her story?

Your Walk with God

Bible

Schedule three times this week to be alone with God. Each day, read the passage indicated below and answer the questions that follow.

DAY ONE: EPHESIANS 2:1–3

Some of the things I observe in this passage:

One idea for how to apply this passage to my life:

DAY TWO: EPHESIANS 2:4–7

Some of the things I observe in this passage:

One idea for how to apply this passage to my life:

DAY THREE: EPHESIANS 2:8–10

Some of the things I observe in this passage:

One idea for how to apply this passage to my life:

Prayer

Each day, pray for two people in your group. Ask God to help them learn to tell their stories effectively to the people on their Impact List in the days ahead.

Scripture Memory

Memorize this verse this week:

> For Christ also suffered once for sins, the righteous for the unrighteous, to bring you to God (1 Peter 3:18).

On Your Own: Reflections on the Essential Message of Christianity

In the next session, we will explore several different ways to share the basics of the gospel with others. To prepare for the study, go through the following worksheet and jot down a few notes about the steps you would use and some illustrations you could tell that would explain the gospel and how someone could become a Christian.

1. God's main reason for creating human beings was . . .

2. Even though God loves us, the reason human beings are not in his kingdom is . . .

3. Just trying to live a good life is not enough to bridge the gap between us and God because . . .

4. While sincerity is a good quality, the reason it is not enough to get us back to God is . . .

5. The solution to life's biggest problems that Christianity offers—and is unlike what all other world religions teach—is . . .

6. The reasons we should believe Christianity is truly from God and not just another human-devised faith system is . . .

7. The difference between being a church member and being a true Christian is . . .

8. The main thing Jesus wants those who do not know him to understand is . . .

9. The most common misunderstandings people have about Christianity are . . .

10. Although Christians and Christian leaders make mistakes, the reason Christianity is true and should be believed is . . .

11. *Grace* is central to Christianity and is defined as . . .

12. The steps I took—and that every person must take—to become a Christian are . . .

13. The consequence of ignoring the gospel message and refusing the kindness God offers in Christ is . . .

PRESENTING THE MESSAGE

PERSONAL STUDY: 1 Corinthians 1;
2 Corinthians 2:1–16
SCRIPTURE MEMORY: Titus 3:5; Ephesians 2:8–9
ON YOUR OWN: Tough Questions

"Everyone has a 'personal relationship with God' already: either as a condemned criminal standing before a righteous judge or as a justified co-heir with Christ and adopted child of the Father."

—Michael S. Horton

Making the Message Clear

You are at home waiting for a phone call from a business client. After sitting idle for several hours, you decide to work in the garage for a few minutes. When you return, your seven-year-old son reports that a man called you.

Excitedly, you ask your son what he said. But he can't remember any details. He forgot to write down the phone number where the man could be contacted. Although he remembers something about needing to sign some contract, he can't remember what the terms were. As hard as your son is trying, the most he can get across is that "he was a nice man"—but all the other relevant information is lost from your son's memory.

Christians who don't know how to communicate the gospel clearly are a lot like that seven-year-old. They have good intentions, and they feel "Jesus was a nice man," but if they don't know how to share the nuts and bolts of the gospel message, they can't help the people who need the message relayed. Even worse, they may confuse and frustrate people.

This study will show you how to explain the basics of the gospel in a simple and effective manner. It will also help you clarify your personal story of conversion and the message that converted you. We will begin by looking at four essentials of the gospel message.

Essential #1: *God*

1. *Read 2 Thessalonians 1:6.* How would you explain to a nonbeliever the fact that God is fair and just?

2. *Turn to 1 Peter 1:15–16.* How would you describe to a nonbeliever the concept of God's holiness?

3. *Read 1 John 4:16.* What is another way to describe to a nonbeliever the idea that "God is love"?

Essential #2: *People*

4. According to Romans 3:23, how does God regard the human condition?

5. *Read Romans 5:12.* What are the consequences of our sin?

Essential #3: *Christ*

6. *Turn to John 1:14.* What does this verse say Christ did to end the separation between God and people?

7. According to 1 Peter 3:18, what was the result of Jesus' sacrifice for us?

Essential #4: *You*

8. *Read Acts 3:19.* What did Peter say occurs when a person responds to the gospel message?

9. What does God promise in 1 John 1:9 when a person confesses his or her sins and turns to God for forgiveness?

Five Illustrations to Help Clarify the Message

The following are five simple illustrations you can use to help you clarify the gospel message when you are sharing with another person.

Illustration 1: DO Versus DONE

This simple verbal illustration describes the difference between religion and Christianity:

> *Religion is spelled D-O. It's the plan most people are on—trying to do enough to earn God's favor, and trying to do enough to feel good about themselves. It centers on what we accomplish and on our efforts. Ultimately, it reduces the hope for salvation—if we ever get it (and we can never be sure with this plan)—to being a reward for our own achievements.*
>
> *Christianity is spelled D-O-N-E. It centers on what Christ has done for us. In this plan, he accomplishes something we never could. He pays the price for our sins so they are no longer an issue between us and God. The work Christ did is finished, done. The work we try to do to be forgiven is fruitless, so we admit we are done—and trust instead in him. God now offers us his forgiveness and his leadership. When we accept it, the case for our condemnation is closed—our salvation is achieved through what he has done. (For more information on this illustration, see Paul Little's book How to Give Away Your Faith.)*

10. Why do you think people are so inclined to believe they are responsible for their salvation?

11. How do you think the people on your Impact List would respond to this illustration?

Illustration 2: The Bridge

This simple illustration has been widely published in various forms. We recommend using it with as little detail as possible—you can always say more as you need to or as the person is open to it. Explain it in stages as you draw it. Note that we've merged it with the "DO versus DONE" illustration above.

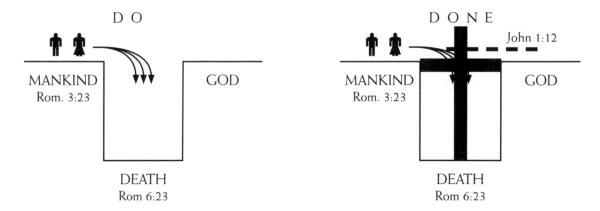

- A gulf exists between people and God.
- Our efforts fall short.
- The result is spiritual death.
- A bridge now exists—it's Christ.
- We can cross over to God and not be condemned to death.
- All we need to do is receive him, because the work has been done.

12. What do you find appealing about the bridge illustration as an evangelistic tool?

13. How do you think the people on your Impact List would respond to this illustration?

Illustration 3: Xs and Os

This illustration (originally used in a sermon by Bill Hybels) portrays the tendency that many people have to think of salvation as a balancing act between sins and good deeds. They imagine that if they pile up "good deeds" while minimizing bad ones, they'll go to heaven. The underlying assumption here is that God grades on the curve. "After all," such a person might say, "if God won't let someone like me in, who *can* make it into heaven?"

Problems:

- One X is too many (see James 2:10).
- Our Os fall short of God's standard (see Isaiah 64:6).
- Jesus' sacrifice on the cross would be unnecessary if we could please God with our own righteous acts. Yet Jesus said his life was offered as a ransom for many (see Matthew 20:28).

The good news is that God has done for us what we could not do for ourselves. The following illustration shows what happens when we trust in Christ for salvation.

Results:

- God canceled out our *Xs* by sending his Son to take our death penalty for us.
- Not only did Jesus die to take away our *Xs*, but he also offers us his righteousness—his perfect *Os*.
- God offers us the opportunity of salvation as a gift—we must respond and take it.

14. Why do you think the idea of *Xs* and *Os* is such a common fallacy among nonbelievers?

15. How do you think the people on your Impact List would respond to this illustration?

Illustration 4: The Romans Road

If someone is familiar with the Bible and respects its authority, you can help that person see what the Bible says about the plan of salvation. This illustration won't convince the skeptic, but it will make clear what God's Word says about our condition.

1. Romans 3:23: *"For all have sinned and fall short of the glory of God."*
   - This verse clears up any misinformed notions that some people have that they don't need help.
   - It also points out that the standard is God's glory, not our relative position compared to other people.

2. Romans 6:23: *"For the wages of sin is death, but the gift of God is eternal life in Christ Jesus our Lord."*
   - This verse explains the consequences of our sin.
   - It points out what God has done.
   - It emphasizes the centrality of Christ.

3. Romans 10:9: *"If you declare with your mouth, 'Jesus is Lord,' and believe in your heart that God raised him from the dead, you will be saved."*
   - This verse shows the need for a personal response.
   - It affirms that the gospel is centered in the person and identity of Jesus.
   - It proclaims the uniqueness of the historical event of the resurrection.
   - It gives assurance of salvation.

16. How do you think the people on your Impact List would respond to this illustration?

Illustration 5: The Judge Illustration

This story helps resolve the tension between our struggle to affirm God's justice in condemning our sin and our desire to know him as a loving Father. It illustrates two important points: (1) a price must be paid for sin, and justice must be served; and (2) God paid the price himself, by his own choice, at a tremendous cost, so there can be no doubt of his love and commitment to us.

A young woman was picked up for speeding. She was ticketed and taken before the judge. The judge read off the citation and said, "Guilty or not guilty?" The woman replied "Guilty." The judge brought down the gavel and fined her $300 or ten days.

Then an amazing thing took place. The judge stood up, took off his robe, walked down around the front, took out his billfold, and paid the fine.

What's the explanation of this?

The judge was her father. He loved his daughter, yet he was a just judge. His daughter had broken the law, and he couldn't simply say to her, "Because I love you so much, I forgive you. You may leave." If he had done that, he wouldn't have been a righteous judge. He wouldn't have upheld the law. But he loved his daughter so much that he was willing to take off his judicial robe and come down in front and represent her as her father and pay the fine.

The illustration pictures to some extent what God did for us through Jesus Christ. We sinned. The Bible says, "The wages of sin is death." No matter how much he loved us, God had to bring down the gavel and say death, because he is a righteous and just God.

And yet, being a loving God, he loved us so much that he was willing to come down off the throne in the form of the man Christ Jesus and pay the price for us, which was Christ's death on the cross.

FROM JOSH MCDOWELL, *MORE THAN A CARPENTER* (WHEATON: TYNDALE HOUSE, 1977), PP. 114–15. REPRINTED BY PERMISSION.

17. How do you think the people on your Impact List would respond to this illustration about the judge?

Clarifying the Message

Imagine that you are giving instructions to a group of campers on the basics of outdoor survival. The topic of your presentation for the afternoon is knot tying. You learned to tie basic knots long ago, and you're quite sure you'll have no problem explaining them.

But when the time comes and your students are standing there with ropes in hand, you can remember only one knot! As you fumble with trying to tie several others, you get more and more frustrated. Each time, though you have a picture of the knot in your mind, you forget exactly how to tie it. It was easy when your scoutmaster taught you, but teaching it to others turns out to be quite another story.

"Telling is not teaching; listening is not learning." This adage is especially true when it comes to explaining the gospel. It is our familiarity with it that makes some of us think we've mastered the truth of this simple but life-saving message. But when we actually try to explain it, we often realize it's foggier in our minds than we thought. However, through practice, we can clear up our confusion and learn to capably express the gospel.

Practice

In this study, you and your group members will get the chance to present the gospel message by using two of the illustrations we examined this week: (1) the bridge illustration and (2) the Xs and Os illustration. You will present each illustration to the group, perhaps field a few questions, and then get the opportunity to hear feedback.

Although you may feel a little nervous or awkward about "being on the spot" before the group, there is no better way to learn to share the gospel than in the safe and instructive environment of your small group. You may never have another opportunity to have knowledgeable, caring people listen to your gospel presentation and help you improve it. So take a risk and trust God to do a work in your life.

At the end of each member's presentation, provide the following feedback:

- You were especially good at . . .
- Your presentation helped me to see this more clearly . . .
- One suggestion for improvement is . . .

Apply It to Your Life

18. What important discovery did you make from this exercise?

Your Walk with God

Bible

Schedule three times this week to be alone with God. Each day, read the passage indicated below and answer the questions that follow.

DAY ONE: 1 CORINTHIANS 1:1–17

Some of the things I observe in this passage:

One idea for how to apply this passage to my life:

DAY TWO: 1 CORINTHIANS 1:18–31

Some of the things I observe in this passage:

One idea for how to apply this passage to my life:

DAY THREE: 2 CORINTHIANS 2:1–16

Some of the things I observe in this passage:

One idea for how to apply this passage to my life:

Prayer

On each of your three days with God this week, pray for the following:

Day One: Spend time praising God. Use Psalm 92 as the text for your meditation.

Day Two: Ask God's forgiveness for those times when you have failed to take advantage of the opportunities he has given you for glorifying him, especially in the area of personal evangelism.

Day Three: Pray for the efforts of at least three group members as they attempt to share the gospel with others.

Scripture Memory

Memorize these verses this week:

He saved us, not because of righteous things we had done, but because of his mercy. He saved us through the washing of rebirth and renewal by the Holy Spirit (Titus 3:5).

For it is by grace you have been saved, through faith—and this is not from yourselves, it is the gift of God—not by works, so that no one can boast (Ephesians 2:8–9).

In the next study, we will learn how to handle the tough questions that non-believers can pose to witnessing Christians. To prepare, it is important that you read the "On Your Own" assignment at the end of this study.

On Your Own: Tough Questions

Have you ever been confronted with a tough question from a skeptical listener? If you have, you know how pressured you feel to come up with an acceptable answer. Christians who share the gospel with others will sometimes run into people who pose challenging questions that test the extent of their knowledge. To prepare you for this eventuality, below are some of the most commonly asked "tough questions" along with thoughtful replies that can help you formulate your own responses.

In the next study, we will explore these questions—and the issues that often lie beneath them—in greater detail.

1. *Can you prove God exists?*

   - The order and design of the universe indicates the presence of an Orderer and Designer.

   - If there are causes and effects in our universe, it seems logical to assume that all effects result ultimately from a first cause, which is by definition what God is (an uncaused being). Otherwise, the universe—which, according to the Big Bang theory had a beginning 13.8 billion years ago—caused itself, which is absurd.

   - Most people seem to have a sense that they fall short of some standard. Where does this sense of goodness or fairness (what C. S. Lewis calls the sense of "fair play") come from, if not from some absolute goodness? God's standard of righteousness seems to pervade the hearts of people despite their attempts to ignore or erase it.

   - God broke into history. Jesus' life, miracles, and resurrection show that God is at work. If he's at work, he must exist!

   - You could also point to the subjective but real experience in your own life. Refer to instances when God has sustained you or answered prayer. Keep in mind that your personal experience alone will not be enough to convince many people, but it is evidence to be considered.

2. *Isn't God just a projection of idealized thinking (that is, we hope such a being exists, so we assume he does)?*

   - This question ignores the possibility that God exists and acts independently of what we may say or think about him.

   - This question leads us back to a point we mentioned earlier—where do we get the notion of a perfect human being? Where does this sense of an ultimate goodness or perfection come from?

   - Atheists must face the opposite but equally forceful possibility—that God *does* exist in spite of their wish that he didn't!

3. *Does it really matter what you believe in, as long as you have faith?*

- You may want to probe this person's understanding of *faith*. If the person defines it as believing in something for purely subjective reasons, that is not biblical faith. Merely believing something doesn't make it true. Christians, on the other hand, base their faith on objective truth. We believe that God appeared to humans in the person of Jesus Christ, that he died for our sins, and that he rose from the dead. These facts are reported to us as a matter of history to be studied. We put faith in those facts; we don't just have *faith* in an abstract sense.

- Sincere people can be sincerely wrong. Faith is only as good as its object. When people have great faith in an unworthy object (such as a cult leader), their faith is harmful to them, not helpful.

4. *How can a good God allow evil people to exist?*

- We should keep in mind that we all have fallen short and, unless we have turned to Christ, we will be judged for those sins. In that sense, we are all evil and deserving of death. If God wiped away all evil tomorrow, who'd be left?

- God wants relationships based on love. This would be impossible if he coerced everyone to follow him. The possibility for evil always exists when his creatures are given a will to express their desires and they choose to do so selfishly.

- God will not always tolerate evil. There will come a day when it will all be wiped away and replaced with the radiance of his presence. (The book of Revelation gives us a glimpse of that future paradise.) Just as you don't judge a novel until you've read the whole book, you can't judge God until you've seen him work out the climax of history.

5. *If Christianity is true, why is the church full of hypocrites?*

- Jesus said that true and false believers would exist side by side until the end (see the parable of the wheat and the weeds in Matthew 13:24–30). To use an analogy, all of us have heard of instances of doctors being sued for malpractice. Yet none of us have decided that the practice of medicine is useless or that we should stop seeing doctors.

- The fact that hypocrisy exists only reinforces the claims of Christ—that we all need a Savior. If Christianity *weren't* true, then you might be able to find a perfect person other than Jesus.

6. *Isn't it arrogant to claim that Christianity is the only way? Aren't all religions merely different paths to God?*

- The religions of the world produce some obvious disparities in the ways they describe God and human beings. Some proclaim that godhood is merely a state of higher consciousness. Others suppose the existence of multiple deities of varying power and personality. Still others see God as an impersonal essence that pervades all matter. The Christian God differs in that he is separate from his creation, infinite, and personal. It becomes obvious that it is nonsense to talk about all paths leading to God, for world religions have sharply contrasting ideas about who or what God is.

- We cannot brush off the fact that Christianity makes exclusive claims. Merely because we may not like the idea that God has provided but one way to salvation does not diminish its truth. C. S. Lewis stated this succinctly in *Mere Christianity*: "As in arithmetic—there is only one right answer to a sum, and all other answers are wrong." Should math be thrown out because it's so narrow? Or should we be grateful that there is a way to evaluate all answers so that the correct one can be discovered (and we're able to disregard the wrong ones)?

- We must consider the claims that Jesus made about himself. In John 14:6 he declared, "I am the way and the truth and the life. No one comes to the Father except through me." Will Jesus' exclusive claims stand up to scrutiny? In light of his resurrection, we believe they do.

7. *Isn't it enough that people lead a good life?*

- Again, we are faced with that crucial matter of what constitutes a *good* life. It is easy to compare ourselves favorably to obvious sinners who have committed heinous crimes. But what God declares about our goodness is quite different. He finds each one of us guilty of sin and unworthy of his presence.

- Even some of the most saintly people we can think of—Mother Teresa and Billy Graham, to name two—called themselves sinners who are undeserving of God's grace. In fact, the only person in history who can truly be called good is Jesus Christ, for he lived a sinless life. How does our goodness compare to his?

- Why attempt to rely on our own efforts to earn God's favor when he has already provided a way out of our dilemma? All we need to do is receive the gift of salvation through Jesus Christ.

8. *What about those who have never heard of Christ? How can God judge them?*

   - No one goes to hell merely for rejecting Christ. We all deserve hell because we're sinners—rejecting Christ would be just one more sin on a long list of other sins.

   - We can be sure that God will judge everyone fairly and righteously. Besides, what God chooses to do with someone who has never heard of Christ is irrelevant to this person's case—because he or she *has* heard the gospel. The question is how that person will respond.

   - We must keep in mind that salvation is a benefit that God bestows on us as a great and precious gift. It is not a "right" the human race has earned.

9. *How can we believe the Bible is from God when it is full of errors?*

   - This question is often a smoke screen. Ask, "What errors in particular concern you?" Frequently, the person won't be able to name even one. Or, if he or she does, it is so general that it's obvious the person is simply trying to hide behind an excuse.

   - A careful examination of the Bible leads to the conclusion that it is a remarkably consistent collection of documents. Its forty authors produced over a span of 1,500 years some very similar ideas about God, the human condition, the person and mission of Jesus Christ, heaven and hell, and our eternal destiny.

- As Mark Twain once observed, it's not the things we don't understand about the Bible that often trouble us—it's the things we do understand.

COPING WITH TOUGH QUESTIONS

PERSONAL STUDY: John 15–16
SCRIPTURE MEMORY: John 1:12
ON YOUR OWN: Scriptural Prayers for Nonbelievers

"The verbal tool of exploring mystery together is . . . dialogue. We subject ourselves to the same questions we pose to others, and as we traverse them together, we may arrive at surprising conclusions we could never have reached when simply trying to defeat one another's logic. . . . The questions stick with us, even haunt us, long after we ask them, and we await insight together. The process is more important than an immediate decision."

—ADAM S. McHUGH

A Humble Defense

Through a horrendous mistake, you have been charged with and indicted for a serious crime. You get some advice and find a lawyer who agrees to defend you for a very modest fee. As the trial begins, you are stunned when your attorney admits to the jury that you have a very weak case. He confesses that he believes you're innocent, but he cannot offer any evidence other than "he feels it's true."

As the trial continues, this attorney passes on all opportunities to cross-examine witnesses and makes no effort to produce evidence in your favor. He just smiles, expecting his good-natured sincerity to convince the jury. You realize you're in big trouble. Even if you try to find another lawyer, you are afraid the damage done by now may be permanent—you may never have another chance to clear your name.

Unfortunately, far too many Christians are like this attorney when it comes to defending their beliefs. We read in Jude 3 that we are to "contend for the faith." In 1 Peter 3:15 we are told to "always be prepared to give an answer to everyone who asks you to give the reason for the hope that you have . . . with gentleness and respect." It is wonderful to know the benefits of Christ, but it is just as important to be able to explain why it makes sense to trust in him. Commonly, this process involves demonstrating *why* Christ is the only way.

Yet we also need to make our defense without arrogance or without the goal of proving that we're right and the other person is wrong. We need to learn how to express our confidence with a humble admission that we all have questions and are not afraid to look to God for answers. Those answers may not come immediately—or the answers we get may raise new questions—but we can allow for a process and trust that God wants us to have satisfied minds as well as hearts.

Defending the faith follows logically from living it. In this study, we will learn how to respond to questions that nonbelievers commonly raise about the Christian faith. We will also learn how to recognize smoke screens that nonbelievers often resort to using as a way of avoiding spiritual truths. As you work through this study on apologetics, don't view it as a "cram session" for the work ahead. Don't be lulled into thinking you've mastered everything there is to know about the subject!

Instead, make it your goal to always keep learning more facts about the Christian faith and to discover new, more effective ways of answering difficult questions. Be curious about things you thought you knew, but realize when your previous "answers" do not hold up to further scrutiny. Read books that will help you respond to a critic's challenges and keep you on a quest to allow for your own "inner skeptic" to wonder about questions you still have. Remember that learning about and representing Christ better is a lifelong journey.

Tough Questions

1. What are some questions about Christianity you've been asked that you wished you had better answers for?

2. What do you think are some of the questions the people on your Impact List have?

Common Questions Nonbelievers Ask

If you read the "On Your Own" assignment from last week, you already have a good grounding about the kinds of questions nonbelievers frequently ask about Christianity. It may be surprising to learn there are actually only a handful of basic questions people ask, though they can be phrased in a variety of ways. In fact, all the questions you come up with will probably be addressed this week!

For this study, we will restate the questions from last week's assignment. For each question, you and your group will then propose a variety of responses. Often, the wisdom of the group is sufficient to formulate a convincing answer. If you need help, feel free to turn to last week's assignment for ideas.

3. How might you respond to someone who asks, "How can you prove God exists?"

4. How would you respond to the following statement: "God is merely the projection of idealized thinking"?

5. What answer would you give to someone who asks you, "Why can't I believe anything I want as long as I believe it sincerely?"

6. If somebody declared to you, "I can't believe in God because he allows evil people to exist," what response could you offer?

7. What response could you give to the question, "If Christianity is genuine, then why is the church full of hypocrites?"

8. Respond to the following question: "How can Christians claim their religion is the only way to God?"

9. What would you say to someone who told you he or she was going to heaven because of living a good life?

10. How would you respond to someone who asked, "What about those who have never heard of Christ? How can God judge them?"

11. What would you say to someone who told you that he or she couldn't believe in Christianity because the Bible was full of errors?

12. Which of these questions would you be most likely to hear from a person on your Impact List?

Detecting Smoke Screens

Some people ask questions not because they want answers but because they want an excuse *not* to believe. They are often more interested in inventing clever questions to confound Christians than they are in seeking earnestly after the truth. It is important to learn how to get around these evasions so you can get to the heart of the issue—that person's standing before God and need of salvation through Christ.

13. What "symptoms" might you notice in someone who was using difficult questions as a smoke screen?

14. How should you handle people who appear to have other motives for asking the questions that they do?

15. You will on occasion meet people who consider themselves Christians but are in fact not. These people have some knowledge of spiritual matters. They may attend church and pray. But as you question them, it will become apparent they do not understand the importance of making a decision to accept Christ. It's harder to deal with them because they're making assumptions about themselves that they shouldn't. How would you respond if such a person said, "I've been in the church all my life. Why do you talk to me as if I don't have Christ when he's been with me and I've prayed to him all my life?"

Leading Someone Across the Line

If you sense that a person has been convicted by the gospel message, you should be prepared to lead him or her to Christ. We suggest using the following method.

Asking Leading Questions

Step One: Ask, "Have you ever personally received Christ, or are you still on the journey?"

16. What advantage do you see in phrasing the question this way rather than asking simply, "Have you been saved?"

Step Two: If the person wants to receive Christ, terrific! (There are some additional suggestions later in this study for guiding a person through this essential step.) If they are not ready, ask, "How far along the path are you?"

17. What do you think asking the question, "How far along the path are you?" accomplishes?

Step Three: Conclude by asking, "Would you like to become a Christian and be sure of it?" Or, "Is there anything standing in the way of your asking Christ into your life?"

18. What do you think is accomplished by asking these concluding questions?

How to Pray with a Person to Receive Christ

There are three basic ways to pray with someone who is ready to receive Christ:

- *Have the person pray out loud in his or her own words.* Tell the person to admit his or her sin to God and to ask Christ to take over his or her life.
- *Pray out loud and have the person repeat your words.* Don't put the person on the spot. As you pray, avoid stuffy, formal language. Pray as if you were the person (that is, say, "I want to invite you into my life, Jesus").
- *Have the person pray on his or her own later.* Follow up the next day to see if the person did pray and what it was that he or she actually prayed.

When you pray, emphasize these three ideas:

- *Jesus forgives us.* He restores our standing before God and erases all sin—past, present, and future. In effect, we are living from this day forward with a clean slate.
- *Jesus leads us.* Christ not only forgives us but also wants to lead us and direct our lives on an adventure that will last a lifetime.
- *Jesus is worthy of our thanks.* When a person prays to receive Christ, something of eternal significance happens. We may or may not have an emotional response, but the results are still the same. Christ is worthy of being appreciated at this significant moment.

Apply It to Your Life

19. In light of the information shared in this study, what might you do differently the next time you witness to someone?

Your Walk with God

Bible

Schedule three times this week to be alone with God. Each day, read the passage indicated below and answer the questions that follow.

DAY ONE: JOHN 15:1–17

Some of the things I observe in this passage (especially as they pertain to evangelism):

One idea for how to apply this passage to my life:

DAY TWO: JOHN 15:18–16:15

Some of the things I observe in this passage (especially as they pertain to evangelism):

One idea for how to apply this passage to my life:

DAY THREE: JOHN 16:16–33

Some of the things I observe in this passage (especially as they pertain to evangelism):

One idea for how to apply this passage to my life:

Prayer

On each of your three days with God this week, pray for the following:

Day One: Pray for God's wisdom as you seek to answer the questions people will ask as you witness to them. Pray for an opportunity to use what you've learned.

Day Two: Offer a prayer of thanksgiving for those people on your Impact List who have been receptive to your spiritual inquiries or have even accepted Christ.

Day Three: Pray for the efforts of your group members as they continue to share the gospel with the people on their Impact List.

Scripture Memory

Memorize this verse this week:

> *Yet to all who did receive him, to those who believed in his name, he gave the right to become children of God* (John 1:12).

In the next study, we will consider the vital role that prayer plays in our attempts to win others to Christ and will review necessary skills that will help us extract the most from our Bible study. To prepare, ask yourself what value you think prayer has for those who don't know Christ.

On Your Own: Scriptural Prayers for Nonbelievers

Sometimes, you might feel at a loss for specific things you can pray for when you think of your unsaved friends and loved ones. The following are a few scriptural guidelines you can use to fill in that gap. Before your next group meeting, use these topics (adapted from *Discipleship Journal* magazine, issue 34) to pray for the people on your Impact List.

- Pray for God to draw them to himself and break the unhealthy ties they have to anything other than him. *"No one can come to me unless the Father who sent me draws them"* (John 6:44).
- Pray that they would seek to know God and become dissatisfied with all the other things that occupy their attention. *"But if from there you seek the LORD your God, you will find him if you seek him with all your heart and with all your soul"* (Deuteronomy 4:29).
- Pray for them to believe the Scriptures and be able to trust its claims. *"Faith comes from hearing the message, and the message is heard through the word about Christ"* (Romans 10:17).
- Pray that Satan would be prevented from blinding them to the truth. *"The god of this age has blinded the minds of unbelievers, so that they cannot see the light of the gospel that displays the glory of Christ, who is the image of God"* (2 Corinthians 4:4).
- Pray for the Holy Spirit's work to affect their sense of self-sufficiency and self-righteousness, and then lead them away from error to the truth. *"When he [the Holy Spirit] comes, he will prove the world to be in the wrong about sin and righteousness. . . . But when he, the Spirit of truth, comes, he will guide you into all the truth"* (John 16:8, 13).
- Pray that they would be receptive to Jesus' words and believe in him as Savior. *"Very truly I tell you, whoever hears my word and believes him who sent me has eternal life"* (John 5:24).

- Pray that they would feel remorse and anger about their sin and turn from it to God. *"Repent, then, and turn to God, so that your sins may be wiped out"* (Acts 3:19).

- Pray that they would confess Christ as Lord, acknowledging the resurrection as the cornerstone of what God has done to prove Christianity is true— and then unashamedly declare their love for and submission to him. *"If you declare with your mouth, 'Jesus is Lord,' and believe in your heart that God raised him from the dead, you will be saved. For it is with your heart that you believe and are justified, and it is with your mouth that you profess your faith and are saved"* (Romans 10:9–10). *"If anyone is ashamed of me and my words in this adulterous and sinful generation, the Son of Man will be ashamed of them when he comes in his Father's glory"* (Mark 8:38).

- Pray that they would take root and grow in Christ, continuing to live in grateful connection with him for the rest of their lives. *"So then, just as you received Christ Jesus as Lord, continue to live your lives in him, rooted and built up in him, strengthened in the faith as you were taught, and overflowing with thankfulness"* (Colossians 2:6–7).

TIME OUT FOR PRAYER

PERSONAL STUDY: 2 Timothy 1–4
SCRIPTURE MEMORY: Ephesians 6:18; 2 Timothy 2:15
ON YOUR OWN: How to Finish Well

"What people pray for will tell you more than anything else whether they are locked into the vision and priorities of the church."

—ANDY STANLEY

The Role of Prayer in Evangelism

Can you imagine any evangelist saying that for the purposes of helping people understand the gospel, we can pray if we want to, but it is not really that important? We need to have the Holy Spirit's power at work in us as we share our faith, and those listening need his work so they can understand and overcome their spiritual blindness.

The Holy Spirit's role in evangelism is of great importance. His convicting work goes before us to prepare hearts to receive the good news of salvation in Christ (see John 16:8–11). His enabling and teaching give us words of wisdom that can answer questions and enlighten those with whom we speak (see Luke 12:11–12; John 14:26;

16:13). He is the One who ultimately convinces people of the true identity and significance of the person of Jesus Christ (see 1 Corinthians 12:3). He is the One who seals us in him at the point of conversion (see 1 Corinthians 12:13; Ephesians 1:13). When we consider all that the Holy Spirit accomplishes for us, can we afford *not* to pray for God's leadership as we strive to reach others with the gospel?

The focus of this meeting will be to reflect on the lessons you have learned about evangelism so far and to bring requests before God in prayer. You will also review everything you have mastered about Bible study and application. It should be a rewarding time of sharing and learning with the group of people who have come to mean so much to you.

1. What are two benefits you have received from this study on personal evangelism?

2. What aspect of the gospel have you come to appreciate in a new way through this study?

3. What misconceptions about evangelism have you managed to correct as a result of this study?

4. What insight about one of the group members have you gained by watching and listening to his or her testimony and presentation of the gospel?

5. What successes or frustrations have you encountered so far in your attempts to share the gospel with the people on your Impact List?

6. If you are to continue to apply what you've learned in this study of evangelism, in what specific ways will you need prayer?

Approved Workers

Some of the great leaders of history have concluded their reign or term in office with a farewell address. While the apostle Paul didn't have the opportunity to give a farewell address to his coworkers in Christ, he did have the chance to record some final instructions to one of his coworkers as he awaited execution in a Roman prison. We know it as the book of 2 Timothy.

This was most likely the last letter written by Paul, and it can be seen as his farewell address to the generations of leaders who would follow him. It is therefore fitting that we study this letter of parting wisdom, for in a very short time this small-group experience will be ending. It is our hope that during the course of *The Way of a Disciple* and *The Work of a Disciple* you have learned a great deal, not only about understanding the Bible but also about how to apply that wisdom to your life.

Paul's Final Letter

7. How would you describe Paul's disposition, especially considering the circumstances in which he found himself (see 2 Timothy 1:1–18)?

8. What specific encouragement did Paul give Timothy in this chapter that you need to hear for yourself right now?

9. How is a Christian like a solider, an athlete, and a farmer (see 2:1–7)?

10. Looking back over the course of your participation in this small group, how has your attitude toward obedience and suffering changed?

11. What are some characteristics of a worker approved by God (see 2:8–18)?

12. What such qualities have you seen flourishing in the person sitting to your right?

13. What makes it hard to pursue the qualities of a mature believer (see 2:19–26)?

14. What has hindered you from pursuing the characteristics God wants to develop in you?

15. How would you describe a person who has given himself or herself over to natural desires (see 3:1–9)?

16. In what ways have you seen the people on your Impact List burdened by the sins Paul describes in the passage?

17. What do you observe about Paul's regard for Scripture (see 3:14–17)?

18. In what ways has your regard for the importance of Scripture changed during the course of this small group?

19. How would you summarize the charge that Paul gave to Timothy (see 4:1–8)?

20. What would have made it hard for you to fulfill the same charge?

21. What do you observe about Paul's relationships with various coworkers in Christ (see 4:9–22)?

22. Write out a brief one- or two-sentence statement for each group member about what you will miss about him or her when the group ends.

Group Prayer

Take some time to pray together with your group about the task of evangelism in the world. This prayer time will probably last from 30 to 45 minutes, depending on the number of people in your group and how long they each pray. It is important for you and your group members to recognize the link between prayer and evangelism, for both are essential to the expansion of the church in the world. When it is clear that everyone has had an opportunity to bring his or her requests before the Father, close with a short word of thanks.

Your Walk with God

Bible

Schedule three times this week to be alone with God. Each day, read the passage indicated below and answer the questions that follow.

DAY ONE: 2 TIMOTHY 1:1–2:13

Some of the things I observe in this passage:

One idea for how to apply this passage to my life:

DAY TWO: 2 TIMOTHY 2:14–3:9

Some of the things I observe in this passage:

One idea for how to apply this passage to my life:

DAY THREE: 2 TIMOTHY 3:10–4:22

Some of the things I observe in this passage:

One idea for how to apply this passage to my life:

Prayer

On each of your three days with God this week, pray for the following:

Day One: Say a prayer of adoration. Think of five attributes of God that are worthy of your praise.

Day Two: Pray for at least three of the people in your group. Also continue to pray for the people on your Impact List.

Day Three: Identify at least three benefits you've experienced from being in this small group and spend time thanking God for providing them for you.

Scripture Memory

Memorize these verses this week:

> *Pray in the Spirit on all occasions with all kinds of prayers and requests. With this in mind, be alert and always keep on praying for all the Lord's people* (Ephesians 6:18).

> *Do your best to present yourself to God as one approved, a worker who does not need to be ashamed and who correctly handles the word of truth* (2 Timothy 2:15).

On Your Own: How to Finish Well

As you come to the conclusion of this curriculum, it may be helpful to consider the question of endings in general. *How does someone finish well?* Life is full of endings you must navigate:

- You set a goal for yourself, and you finally achieve it.
- The sports season is over, and the team disbands until next year.
- Your steady job has ended, and you are going on to what's next (by your choice or someone else's).
- You're about to move to a new city, and you now have to say good-bye to neighbors and friends.
- A relationship has reached a point of impasse, and you've decided to go your separate ways.
- You get a report from the doctor, and you must now face life's final transition.

Hard as it may be to admit, most of us don't do endings well. We may not know what to do at such times, or we try things that just don't seem to work and leave us feeling incomplete. We also may have strong emotions like anger, fear, or sadness, and these are so uncomfortable that we go into denial so we don't have to face the pain.

To help you as you bring this study to a close, here are some tips on how to make an end that maximizes the good while minimizing the negative.

Every Gain Includes a Loss, and Every Loss Includes a Gain

There is no such thing as a situation that is only *gain* or only *loss*. Every gain means you give up something, and vice versa. This is easy to overlook when you go from something you deem to be *negative* to something you deem *positive*.

For example, if you have been unemployed and finally get a job, it may seem like that's only a gain. But something is lost as well: the discretion you had to use your time as you chose is now gone, and your new employer will now be dictating the bulk of your best hours each week. Many other good things also have a downside. Gaining a spouse means losing your ability to live independently. Having a child means losing many of your freedoms so you can care for the life with whom you've been entrusted. Growing up and stepping out into adult freedom means losing your dependence on your parents. Getting a raise means more responsibility and less freedom to fail. The examples are endless.

William Bridges, in his book *Transitions: Making Sense of Life's Changes*, reminds us "endings make beginnings possible." So accept the ending that opens the door to every new beginning. *Find the gain in every loss, but also be aware of the loss in every gain.*

Every Significant Change in Life Includes an Emotional Component

Sometimes, when you are in the midst of exciting changes, it can be easy to overlook the need to *feel all your feelings* in the midst of those changes. The new reality may be so gripping you forget to notice how you feel—but while there is obvious excitement in what has come to pass, there is also unacknowledged sadness at the losses. For this reason, you will do well to acknowledge the range of feelings that accompany an ending and not deny those feelings.

The good thing about feeling feelings is that you can feel them to completion. If you deny those feelings, however, they pop up later and go unresolved, causing problems down the line. So *notice what you are feeling and allow those emotions to be without judging them.*

How You End Something with Others Is How They Will Remember You

When you leave a job, a neighborhood, or a team, your last words and actions will be how you will be remembered. You cannot undo a bad ending, even if you did a lot of good before. But paradoxically, if you end well, people will tend to be more forgiving and more likely to see your prior mistakes in light of the positive way you exited. So, for example, giving your boss or fellow employees a tongue-lashing when you exit is a bad idea, because whatever you've done prior to that will be colored by the poor impressions you made on our way out. *Put your best foot forward—and don't kick back—as you head out any door.*

225

Change Helps to Remove the Illusion of Control

God made the world in an ever-changing, fluctuating way, and no solid or unchanging situation exists in this world. In spite of this, many of us still spend our lives trying to set up such reliable circumstances or relationships. Every ending reminds us we can never take anything or anyone for granted. We must enjoy what we have while we have it, and let go when it is time to let go.

Don't build a foundation on things that cannot support you, and don't fall for the illusion that you can ever set up a job, a friendship, a home, or a way of life that will enable you to feel "settled." Remember that the only thing that never changes is the certainty of change. For this reason, *hold fast to the changelessness of God so you can let go gracefully and gratefully.*

Commit to "Closure Conversations" Without Regrets

Rather than avoiding the hard conversations that an ending often precipitates, step into them with forethought. Consider those things you will *regret not saying* to bring completion to the relationship and those things you *will regret saying* to "get off your chest." Remember the words of Proverbs 13:3: "Those who speak rashly will come to ruin."

Make a list of the things you want to say and how you might say them well, with no regrets, and write in your journal the things best left unsaid. Acknowledge that you might *want* to say these words, but you choose keep them to yourself. As Proverbs 17:28 states, "Even fools are thought wise if they keep silent." *Say what needs to be said with wisdom, grace, and courage—and leave the rest unsaid.*

Look Back, Look Forward, Look Around, and Look Up

Every ending is a chance to *look back.* What did you learn from the experience? What makes you feel grateful? How have you changed? An ending is also a chance to *look forward.* What's next? What might you want to do differently? What kind of person do you want to be in the next situation you find yourself in?

Also, when an ending happens, *look around* you. Who is still in your life you can count on (at least for now)? What good gifts do you still have, even though change is coming? What have you done that you can be proud of? Finally, at every ending, *look up.* Where is God in all this? What is he teaching you? How can you become even more reliant on his unchanging nature in the midst of life's uncertainties?

Noticing these things and taking stock of them can make an ending much more easeful and formative. So, *keep your eyes wide open. Be curious, grateful, and hopeful. And trust God with the inevitable uncertainties.*

The Apostle Paul's Example

To conclude, consider the following summary of how the apostle Paul chose to end his time with the believers in Ephesus:

> *From Miletus, Paul sent to Ephesus for the elders of the church. When they arrived, he said to them: "You know how I lived the whole time I was with you, from the first day I came into the province of Asia. I served the Lord with great humility and with tears and in the midst of severe testing by the plots of my Jewish opponents. You know that I have not hesitated to preach anything that would be helpful to you but have taught you publicly and from house to house. I have declared to both Jews and Greeks that they must turn to God in repentance and have faith in our Lord Jesus.*
>
> *"And now, compelled by the Spirit, I am going to Jerusalem, not knowing what will happen to me there. I only know that in every city the Holy Spirit warns me that prison and hardships are facing me. However, I consider my life worth nothing to me; my only aim is to finish the race and complete the task the Lord Jesus has given me—the task of testifying to the good news of God's grace.*
>
> *"Now I know that none of you among whom I have gone about preaching the kingdom will ever see me again. Therefore, I declare to you today that I am innocent of the blood of any of you. For I have not hesitated to proclaim to you the whole will of God. Keep watch over yourselves and all the flock of which the Holy Spirit has made you overseers. Be shepherds of the church*

of God, which he bought with his own blood. I know that after I leave, savage wolves will come in among you and will not spare the flock. Even from your own number men will arise and distort the truth in order to draw away disciples after them. So be on your guard! Remember that for three years I never stopped warning each of you night and day with tears.

"Now I commit you to God and to the word of his grace, which can build you up and give you an inheritance among all those who are sanctified. I have not coveted anyone's silver or gold or clothing. You yourselves know that these hands of mine have supplied my own needs and the needs of my companions. In everything I did, I showed you that by this kind of hard work we must help the weak, remembering the words the Lord Jesus himself said: 'It is more blessed to give than to receive.'"

When Paul had finished speaking, he knelt down with all of them and prayed. They all wept as they embraced him and kissed him. What grieved them most was his statement that they would never see his face again. Then they accompanied him to the ship (Acts 20:17–38).

Today, think about why this is a great example of a leader finishing his time with his flock well, what you can learn from what he said, and what you can take away from the way that he said these final words to them.

MAKING A DIFFERENCE IN YOUR WORLD

If you have completed all the studies in *The Way of a Disciple* and *The Work of a Disciple* (volumes 1 and 2 in the *Walking with God Series*), you and your fellow group members have been travelers on a long journey. In some ways, it is now over. Although you will all still be friends after the meetings end, the relationships you have enjoyed will now begin to change. It is just inevitable once these regular meetings cease.

But in other ways, it is not over. You will probably see each other from time to time. Truths that you are applying to your lives will continue to transform you. The experiences you have shared together, though in the past, have changed you—and will remain with you always. Before you embark on the separate journeys that God has determined for each of you, take one final look at the essential truths you have learned in Part 3, "Making a Difference in Your World."

Reflect on What You've Learned

1. Why is personal evangelism an important part of the Christian life?

2. How would you describe your evangelistic style?

3. How has your approach to evangelism changed as a result of this study?

4. How would you describe the main points of the gospel?

5. Why is prayer important for evangelism?

Reviewing the Four Challenges

6. *A disciple is one who . . . walks with God.* Why is it important to stay attached to God (see John 15:4–5)?

7. What are the results of a steady walk with God (see Colossians 2:5–7)?

8. *A disciple is one who . . . lives the Word.* What does the Word of God do for your mind (see Romans 12:1–2)?

9. How would you characterize someone in whom the Word of God dwells richly (see Colossians 3:16–17)?

10. How can studying the Word bring you to spiritual maturity (see Hebrews 5:13–14)?

11. *A disciple is one who . . . contributes to the work.* For what purpose are you to use the gifts that God has given you (see Ephesians 4:11–13)?

12. How are you to work in the service that God has called you to do (see Colossians 1:28–29)?

13. What importance should you attach to your participation in the body of Christ (see Hebrews 10:24–25)?

14. *A disciple is one who . . . impacts the world.* What does it mean to be salt and light to the world (see Matthew 5:13–14)?

15. In your own words, how did Jesus describe the need for evangelism (see Matthew 9:36–38)?

16. What words did Paul use to describe the effective witness for Christ (see Colossians 4:5–6)?

From this point on, you're on your own! Keep up your regular habit of Bible study, prayer, and Scripture memory.

The Way of a Disciple

The Way of a Disciple

Don Cousins and Judson Poling

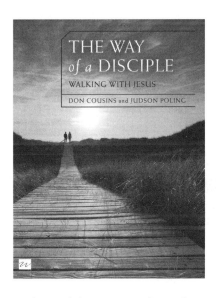

At its core, Christianity is not so much knowing about Jesus' teachings as it is about knowing him. As a believer in Christ, you embrace him as a person, not merely as a doctrine or philosophy. You form a relationship with the living God and become his disciples as you walk with him, live the Word, contribute to his work, and seek to impact your world.

The two volumes in the *Walking with God Series* have been written to help you and your small-group members put these practices into action and become disciples of Jesus. In this first volume, you will discover the God who loves you, see how he sought you out, and understand how he desires to know you as a friend. You will look at the preparation God made to send Jesus into the world, see Christ's words and works, and explore the wonder of his majesty and tender compassion. You will also examine the sacrifice Jesus made for your sins and learn what it means to follow him as Lord day by day.